# CREDIT UNIONS

## in the United Kingdom

# CREDIT UNIONS

## in the United Kingdom

**RICHARD BERTHOUD**
**and TERESA HINTON**

Policy Studies Institute

© Policy Studies Institute, 1989

**PSI Publications are obtainable from all good bookshops, or by visiting the Institute at 100 Park Village East, London NW1 3SR (01-387 2171).**

**Sales Representation: Pinter Publishers Ltd.**

**Individual and Bookshop orders to: Marston Book Services Ltd, PO Box 87, Oxford, OX4 1LB.**

A CIP catalogue record of this book is available from the British Library

PSI Research Report 693

ISBN 0 85374 405 X

Laserset by Policy Studies Institute

Printed in Great Britain by BPCC Wheatons Ltd, Exeter

# Contents

# Acknowledgements

This enquiry into the work of credit unions in the United Kingdom was supported by the Joseph Rowntree Memorial Trust. It contributes to a PSI programme of research on the uses of credit and the problems of debt among low income families. The programme has benefited from a series of grants from the JRMT, and we are grateful to the Trustees for their support.

Within the Institute, the research was the joint responsibility of Richard Berthoud and Teresa Hinton. Teresa Hinton carried out much of the fieldwork and supervised a team of local interviewers. Rosemary Lewin, Karin Erskine, Clare Pattinson and Christine Telford also worked directly on the project.

We are grateful to the Registries of Friendly Societies in London and Belfast, the Irish League of Credit Unions, the Association of British Credit Unions and the National Federation of Credit Unions for their cooperation and encouragement. But most of this report is based on interviews with officers and members of individual credit unions, and we are especially grateful for their contributions.

# Introduction

A credit union is a cooperative society offering its members loans out of the pool of savings built up by the members themselves. A union is formed by a group of people with a common interest or 'bond' – working for the same employer, living in the same area or belonging to the same church, club or ethnic group. By agreeing to save regularly they build up a fund from which they can borrow at favourable interest rates. The interest on loans provides the union with an income to cover administrative expenses; any surplus is returned to members in the form of a dividend on savings. The common bond between members is intended to minimise the risk of default on loans. A credit union is a non-profit organisation, controlled by its own membership.

Credit unions aim to encourage savings and to provide members with a source of cheap credit. Many supporters of the concept are particularly keen that these opportunities should be made available to people on low incomes who may have difficulty saving regularly, and who may have limited access to credit from mainstream institutions. Other important objectives include encouragement of good budgeting, and stimulation of a spirit of self-help and community involvement within the group.

Credit unions first developed in Germany and Italy in the 1850s and '60s, but the idea of cooperative credit seems to have taken a different route in this country, leading to the friendly societies and the present day building societies. The movement took hold in North America during the first half of this century, however, and it is from that quarter that credit unions in the United Kingdom have derived much of their inspiration, and some financial support. In the United States there are more than 16,000 credit unions with a membership of

54 million. A credit union loan is one of the commonest ways of borrowing. In Canada one in four adults belongs to a credit union. The World Council of Credit Unions reports more than 10,000 affiliated unions in Africa, and more than 5000 in Asia.

Credit unions are also important in the Republic of Ireland, where 654,000 people belong to 388 unions; and in Northern Ireland, where 99 credit unions have 123,000 members. Membership is estimated to extend to one third of the Catholic population there.

In Great Britain, the 1979 Credit Union Act was intended to stimulate expansion in the number of societies by providing them with a legal framework of their own. There has been some growth, but there are still only 141 credit unions in Great Britain with 35,000 members – that is, less than one member for every 1,000 adults in the population.

The potential advantages of credit unions have been recognised for many years. The Crowther Committee on consumer credit (1971), for instance, saw a 'prima facie' case for their encouragement. The National Consumer Council has been an active advocate, and helped to promote the 1979 legislation. Several local authorities have assisted the growth of credit unions among their constituents with start-up grants or by appointing development workers. And the credit unions themselves have promoted their cause though three umbrella organisations.

Credit unions have attracted interest partly as an example of the wide variety of self-help community groups which have grown up in recent years. But our own starting point was the contrast between two trends in the economic life of the country. There has been unprecedented growth in the use of consumer credit – the real volume of credit doubled between 1980 and 1987. At the same time the gap between rich and poor has widened as a result of high unemployment and growing wage differentials. Previous research has shown that people on low incomes – especially families with children – commonly use credit to manage their cash flow. But these two trends mean one of two things: if the poor are excluded from the expansion of credit, their standard of living may lag even further behind those with more comfortable incomes; but if they have been included in the credit boom, there is a risk of their commitments overreaching their means, and causing serious debt problems.*

---

\* For a review of these issues, see R. Berthoud, *Credit, debt and poverty*, HMSO, 1989.

Credit unions are often advocated as the solution to the credit needs of the poor. This study of credit unions in the United Kingdom was undertaken as a contribution to PSI's programme of research on the uses of credit and problems of debt among low income families.

The research was designed to assess the impact of credit unions in Northern Ireland (where they are common) and in Great Britain (where they are rare) on the savings and credit opportunities of their members; to identify any problems associated with their development; and to reach conclusions about their viability for consumers in general and for low income families in particular.

This has involved:

- describing the location, membership, common bonds and financial structure of all the credit unions in the United Kingdom
- examining the management structures of credit unions, and the operational difficulties they experience.
- finding out who belongs to credit unions and what they gain from their membership.
- assessing the role credit unions play in the context of other savings and credit institutions.
- exploring the implications for the current or future role of credit unions in Great Britain and Northern Ireland.

**Research methods in brief**
Information has been collected in three ways.

(i) *Statistics*: Credit unions are required to submit their audited accounts annually to the Registrars of Friendly Societies in London or Belfast. Details of these accounts were copied and transferred to computer for detailed analysis. In Northern Ireland, these facts were obtained for all credit unions covering the years 1976, 1981 and 1986. For Great Britain, the Annual Returns did not start until 1981, and information was extracted for every year since then.

In Great Britain there were 94 credit unions reigstered at the end of 1986, but we were able to identify and copy complete returns for only 75 of them. Many of those missing from the record were recently formed, and had not, therefore, compiled an account of a full year's work. It is these 75 unions which are used as the base for detailed statistics.

There were also a number of errors and inconsistencies in the accounts (compiled, for the most part, by honorary treasurers with little training). It was possible to identify and correct some of these inconsistencies, but others remain uncorrected because it was not possible to determine the correct version from the information available.

The statistics contributed especially to the description of credit unions in Northern Ireland and Great Britain in Chapter 1.

(ii) *Leader interviews and observation*: Representatives of the three umbrella organisations and of the Registries in London and Belfast were interviewed to help build up a national picture of the activities and problems of credit unions. So were five development workers employed in different parts of Great Britain.

Twelve credit unions were chosen for more detailed investigation. It was not possible to ensure that these formed a strict cross-section of all unions, but they were selected to include representatives of the various categories: in different areas, with different types of common bond, and so on. A researcher visited each of the twelve unions to find out about:

- the history of the credit union;
- its aims and objectives;
- its structure and organisation;
- its problems;
- support from other sources;
- the personal motivations of its leaders;
- their views about wider issues;
- their hopes for the future.

This information was obtained in four ways:

a) *A detailed interview.* One officer knowledgeable about all aspects of the credit union's operation was asked to describe it in detail.

b) *A discussion with officers.* The researcher held a tape-recorded group interview with directors, committee members, treasurers, secretaries and other leaders. 75 out of a possible total of 150 officers took part; 63 of them also filled in a short questionnaire about themselves.

c) *Collection of documentation.* Copies of leaflets and forms used by the credit union were obtained, together with the latest accounts and annual report. In some instances it was also possible to look at research material and/or statistics produced by the credit union itself.

d) *Observation.* The researcher was able to observe a number of the regular credit union collection sessions and to chat informally with members attending them. In some instances this included watching the credit and supervisory committees at work. It was also possible to sit in on two monthly meetings of Boards of Directors and a number of Annual General Meetings.

This work was conducted by one researcher (Teresa Hinton) during the spring and summer of 1987. It is referred to throughout the report, but especially in the analysis of management issues in Chapter 2.

The quotations in this report are taken from direct transcriptions of tape-recordings of group or individual interviews. All names used are entirely fictitious.

Copies of the draft report were sent to all the credit unions participating in the study, so that their comments could be taken into account in the preparation of the final text.

(iii) *Survey of members*: Eight of the credit unions examined in the detailed enquiry just described were asked if they would collaborate in a survey of their members; seven of them agreed.

Within each of the seven, 50 members were selected from the membership lists – half of them from among those with a loan outstanding, half of them without a current loan. Details of the sampling and approach procedures are given in the Appendix, together with a copy of the structured questionnaire. Members were interviewed in person in their own homes. Of the original sample of 350, successful interviews were achieved with 231 – a response rate of 66 per cent. The answers were checked and coded at PSI prior to computer analysis.

This survey provides factual information about the members of credit unions, their employment and income, and their use of other financial institutions, as well as about their use of and feelings about the credit union itself. The findings are quoted especially in the analysis of members and their experiences in Chapters 3, 4 and 5.

There is an important point to be noted about the presentation of the results of the survey. It will be seen that the credit unions differed widely from one to another. This means, first, that there will be some doubt whether the combined results for the seven that happened to be chosen will give a precisely accurate picture of the members of all two hundred unions in the United Kingdom. Second, there is a problem about how they should be combined for analysis. The largest of the seven had thousands of members; the smallest, less than a hundred. In theory, each union's answers should have been given a weight in proportion to its size; but this would have meant the largest swamping the smallest. It was decided instead to allow the diversity between unions to show through by giving exactly equal weight to each. It might be said, therefore, that the members of smaller unions have a disproportionate influence on the results.

## Structure of this report

The first chapter of this report describes the scale of credit union activity in the United Kingdom. We start with the well-established movement in Northern Ireland, before describing the relatively weak but expanding group of unions in Great Britain. The remainder of the report covers both sides of the water. Chapter 2 identifies the leaders of credit unions, and looks at the problems of development and administration from their point of view. Chapter 3 then looks at the ordinary members: what sort of people are they; what do they want from their union; and how much do they participate in its activities? Chapters 4 and 5 are about savings and loans respectively: how do members go about using these services; how does this vary according to their income and other circumstances; how does it compare with their use of building societies, banks, hire purchase and other financial institutions? Chapter 6 examines a problem which faces every credit-giving organisation: how to deal with arrears and bad debts. The final chapter reviews the findings of the research in an attempt to assess the successes and failures of the credit union movement. This leads to some conclusions about what might be done.

## The great debate

Enthusiasts for credit unions in countries all over the world have struggled to reconcile two different objectives of their movement. These aims might be labelled *idealistic* and *instrumental*. The tension between the competing objectives underlies much of the discussion of the development of credit unions in this country, and it is therefore useful to outline the arguments before the detailed results of the research are analysed.

Everyone agrees that credit unions are designed to provide their members with an opportunity to save, and with access to credit on better terms than could be obtained in the open market. The *idealistic* approach wants to achieve more than that. One of the special objectives is to help people with **low incomes** to overcome some of their social and economic disadvantages, especially if they are excluded from or exploited by mainstream financial institutions. A second priority in some parts of the world (though not here) is to deploy union funds within the **local economy**, servicing the cash flow or investment needs of agriculture or small businesses. A third emphasis is on the participation of members in developing and running their own institutions; for some credit unions, the advantages of **'empowerment' and self-help** are at least as important as the narrowly economic benefits of savings and loans.

These *idealistic* considerations imply certain preferences for the organisation of credit unions. They need to be kept small, to ensure that individual members enjoy genuine participation in the management of their own group. The common bond should be based on poor communities, rather than on existing institutions whose members have money to save. Caution is needed to prevent more prosperous members from 'highjacking' the management and/or diverting the union's activities to meet their own requirements. Loans should be made to people who need credit, rather than to those in the best position to repay the money.

The *instrumental* approach is that the provision of a medium of exchange between savings and loans is **an end in itself**. The more people who can enjoy the economic advantages of cheap credit, the better. These advantages are as valuable to people with adequate incomes as to anyone else, and they should be encouraged to join. The most effective common bond from this point of view is the workforce of a particular employer; all the members have regular incomes from which to contribute savings, and regular payments into the union can easily be deducted from earnings. Management objectives of efficiency and financial stability take priority over considerations of procedure or participation.

We are not suggesting that either of these approaches should necessarily be preferred to the other. Many participants in the debate see that both sets of objectives are important, and argue that the practical development of credit unions should be based on a judgement about the relative balance between priorities.

Whatever their relative merits in principle, the lesson from other countries seems to be that the *instrumental* approach is much more successful in practice. In the United States[1], the great majority (77 per cent) of credit unions are based on the workplace; 16 per cent are based on associations of one kind or another, and only 6 per cent have a common bond of residence in a particular locality. Most credit unions serve a cross-section of society with average incomes, rather than the poor. Loans are offered to the 'credit-worthy' rather than the 'credit-needy'. Individual unions have grown larger, and have merged with each other in the search for managerial efficiency and substantial assets. They are administered by professional managers and clerical staff. It is said that the interests of the members have had to take second place to the interests of the institution, in competition with banks and other financial corporations. The same story is told in Canada[2], and in other countries. Much of it is equally true of our own building societies.

All of this is good for the millions of credit union members who enjoy the advantages of regular savings and cheap credit. Prosperous people have access to credit from other sources, though, and it might be asked why credit unions should be especially encouraged if they merely add to the choices available to those without financial problems. In the United States, credit unions have enjoyed tax advantages which are now being called into question. From the idealist point of view, the success of large middle-class unions is seen to undermine the whole point of having credit unions in the first place: enabling the poor to tackle their own disadvantage.

There have been special efforts to promote credit unions for poor communities in North America[3]. In the 1960s the U.S. Office of Economic Opportunity wanted to 'wipe out poverty' by fostering hundreds of credit unions in low-income areas. But the introduction of unions from above, rather than at the initiative of potential members at the 'grass-roots' level, failed to instil the spirit of independence and responsibility necessary for a disciplined and well-administered union. The failure of many of these groups, in spite of grant aid, undermined confidence in the credit union concept. In Canada an 'anti-poverty' credit union failed for much the same reasons[2]. These initiatives suggest that the development of credit unions specially for the poor should be approached with caution. There have nevertheless been some positive experiences in North America from which useful lessons may be drawn.

This report is about experiences in the United Kingdom. The contrast between the *idealistic* and the *instrumental* motivations is not as marked in this country as it is on the other side of the Atlantic, but the tension is there all the same. It is relevant to many of the credit unions' activities described in the following chapters, and to the various other agencies active in the promotion of this form of credit.

## References

1. World Council of Credit Unions, *Statistical Report*, 1986.
2. C. Purden, *Agents for Change: credit unions in Saskatchewan*, Saskatchewan Cooperative Credit Society, Canada, 1980.
3. National Federation of Community Development Credit Unions, *An analysis of the role of credit unions in capital formation and investment in low and moderate income communities*, NFCDCU, United States, 1986.

# 1. Institutions and Finances

**Institutions in Northern Ireland**

Credit unions were first established in Dublin towards the end of the 1950s. By 1960 a credit union had been established in Northern Ireland, in Derry, and in the same year a League was formed to promote, develop and service credit unions in all Ireland. The movement was supported by the Catholic Church on both sides of the border, and by the mid 1960s there were 300 credit unions. The Dail passed the Credit Union Act to regulate operations in the Republic in 1966. Similar legislation was passed in 1969 in Northern Ireland as a sub-section of the Industrial and Provident Societies Act.

The Irish League of Credit Unions (ILCU) today represents 461 credit unions in both the Republic and Northern Ireland. It acts as the representative body and provides a range of support services to its affiliates. These include a central financial service providing short and long-term loans to affiliated groups; insurance for members and employees; model rules; training publications and courses; stationery and an advice service. It also organises 25 regional groupings or Chapters to give a forum to credit union officers for the exchange of information.

Unions affiliated to the Irish League pay 10 per cent of their income into an insurance scheme, and the profits from this provide the revenue with which the League operates its supporting activities. Its income in 1987 was Ir£1,280,000 (UK£1,160,000). The league employs 27 staff, including five field workers.

Credit unions in Northern Ireland are supervised by the Registry of Friendly Societies in Belfast. The legislation governing their operation has recently been brought into line with that in force in Great

Britain with the Credit Unions (Northern Ireland) Order 1985. It does not differ substantially from that operating in the Republic.

The 564,000 credit union members in the Republic of Ireland represent 30 per cent of the adult population. In Northern Ireland, there are 123,000 members – only 12 per cent of all adults. But almost all credit union members are Catholics, and it is estimated that 29 per cent of Catholics in the North belong to a union. This reflects the activity of the Church in promoting credit unions, and credit unions have, until recently, formed their common bonds almost exclusively within Catholic communities.

There has, however, been a recent growth of interest in credit unions among Protestants in Northern Ireland, and across sectarian boundaries. Several unions have been established, or are in course of formation. Some of these have avoided the all Ireland link with the League by joining the National Federation of Credit Unions based in Great Britain.

## Financial structure in Northern Ireland
### Membership
Analysis of the 1986 annual returns shows that the smallest credit union in Northern Ireland had only 200 members. The largest had 12,520:

18 had up to 500 members;
42 had between 501 and 1,000 members;
20 had between 1,001 and 2,000 members;
13 had more than 2,000 members.

The average was 1,240 members – four times the size of the average credit union in Great Britain.

The total number of credit union members in Northern Ireland grew from 78,660 in 1976 to 122,860 in 1986. Only a small proportion of this increase occurred through the formation of new unions: nine unions were formed over the period, attracting an average of 330 members each by 1986. But the 90 existing unions increased their membership by half over the ten years (an average of 430 new members each). The growth was across the board: there was no sign that credit unions which were already relatively large in 1976 grew any faster or slower than those starting from a smaller base.

The growth in numbers was the net result of recruitment keeping ahead of wastage over the years. In 1986, for example, 6,690 people in Northern Ireland left their credit union, but 11,790 joined.

### Assets

The average Northern Ireland credit union had assets of £532,800 at the end of 1986. This works out at £430 for each member: most unions had between £250 and £500 per member, but five had less than £250 and 17 more than £500. The composition of the average balance sheet is shown in Table 1.1.

**Table 1.1    Assets of credit unions in Northern Ireland**

|  | Average per union | Percent of total |
|---|---|---|
| **Assets** | | |
| Loans to members | £428,620 | 80% |
| *less* accumulated provision for bad and doubtful debts | (£12,800) | (2%) |
| Investments | £41,040 | 8% |
| Cash | £34,770 | 7% |
| Fixed assets | £30,480 | 6% |
| Prepayments | £7,840 | 1% |
| Sundry debtors | £2,850 | 1% |
| TOTAL | £532,800 | 100% |
| **Represented by** | | |
| Share capital | £454,340 | 85% |
| General reserve | £47,850 | 9% |
| Unappropriated surplus carried forward | £990 | * |
| Loans due 5+ years | £300 | * |
| Dividends payable | £20,050 | 4% |
| Creditors and charges | £2,830 | 1% |
| Provision for taxation | £2,000 | * |
| Loans and interest | £1,110 | * |
| Balancing item[+] | £3,330 | 1% |
| TOTAL | £532,800 | 100% |

* = less than 0.5%
[+] The balancing item is calculated to ensure that reported assets are all accounted for. It consists of various small items, plus discrepancies in individual unions' accounts.

The great majority of Northern Ireland credit unions' assets were represented by the members' shares built up out of their savings. Credit union legislation sets a general reserve target of 10 per cent of assets, and the figures showed a healthy average of 9 per cent. (There were, however, six credit unions in Northern Ireland whose accounts recorded no general reserve at all; this may have been a mistake in the annual returns.) Most of the assets were in active use in the form of loans to members.

**Table 1.2    Assets of Northern Ireland credit unions, by number of members**

| Number of members | Less than 500 | 500 to 749 | 750 to 999 | 1000 to 1999 | 2000 or more |
|---|---|---|---|---|---|
| Mean assets per member | £370 | £410 | £420 | £390 | £470 |
| *Principal items as percentage of total* | | | | | |
| Due from members | 76% | 68% | 69% | 79% | 87% |
| Investments | 5% | 12% | 16% | 7% | 5% |
| Cash | 11% | 13% | 10% | 5% | 4% |
| Fixed assets | 9% | 8% | 5% | 9% | 4% |
| Share capital | 84% | 84% | 84% | 84% | 87% |
| General reserve | 11% | 10% | 10% | 9% | 8% |
| (No. of unions) | (21) | (27) | (16) | (22) | (13) |

Table 1.2 compares the assets of large and relatively small credit unions in Northern Ireland. It is more interesting for the consistency between categories than for any differences of detail. The largest unions commanded considerable assets: those with 2,000 members or more reported an average of nearly £2 million each. They were also rather wealthier in terms of assets per member than the smallest unions, but there was not a very clear link between size and wealth. Nor were there clear variations in the make-up of total assets: the large unions had naturally devoted larger absolute sums to fixed assets like property or furniture, but this had not eaten into a larger proportion of their capital. Nor had the smaller unions been forced to stretch their resources at the expense of a healthy general reserve. The table shows

a stable pattern which does not suggest that the financial structure of credit unions is crucially affected by their size.

Since assets are accumulated from the regular savings of members, one would expect them to grow over time. Although the figures are broadly consistent with this idea, the pattern of growth is not as strong as might have been expected. The nine unions set up within the last ten years averaged £380 of assets per member, compared with £440 per member among the 90 unions already in existence ten years ago. The ten-year-old unions nearly quadrupled their nominal assets in the period 1976 to 1986; but this growth can be explained entirely in terms of an increase in membership and of inflation. Assets per member were £430 in 1976 (at 1986 prices) and £410 in 1981, compared with £430 in 1986.

## *Income and expenditure*
The average Northern Ireland credit union had an income of nearly £60,000 in 1986 – £50 per member. Almost the whole of the income was derived from interest, mostly from the members in return for their loans:

Since credit unions' income is derived almost entirely from their assets, and assets depend mainly on membership, it follows that income was closely related to membership, with a fairly constant income of about £50 per head for all sizes of union.

**Table 1.3    Income of credit unions in Northern Ireland**

|                                   | Average per union | Percent of total |
|-----------------------------------|-------------------|------------------|
| **Income**                        |                   |                  |
| Interest from loans to members    | £50,430           | 85%              |
| Investment interest               | £4,090            | 7%               |
| Bank interest                     | £2,410            | 4%               |
| Bad debts recovered               | £1,300            | 2%               |
| Other income                      | £1,320            | 2%               |
| TOTAL                             | £59,560           | 100%             |

About half of the average union's income was spent on running costs of one kind or another; the other half was an operating surplus available for distribution or contribution to reserves (Table 1.4).

**Table 1.4    Expenditure of credit unions in Northern Ireland**

|  | Average per union | Percent of total income |
|---|---|---|
| **Expenditure** |  |  |
| Salaries | £7,780 | 13% |
| Loan insurance | £4,250 | 7% |
| Accommodation | £2,860 | 5% |
| Postage, printing, travel etc | £1,810 | 3% |
| Audit and accountancy charges | £1,190 | 2% |
| Other management expenses | £2,630 | 4% |
| Total management expenses | £20,520 | 34% |
| Provision for bad and doubtful debts | £6,380 | 11% |
| Taxation | £1,730 | 3% |
| Depreciation | £1,700 | 3% |
| Other outgoings | £810 | 1% |
| TOTAL EXPENDITURE | £31,140 | 52% |
| **Application of surplus** |  |  |
| Dividend on shares | £19,820 | 33% |
| Rebate of loan interest | £760 | 1% |
| Transfer to reserve (net) | £7,220 | 12% |
| Balancing item[+] | £620 | 1% |
| TOTAL SURPLUS | £28,420 | 48% |
| TOTAL INCOME | £59,560 | 100% |

[+] The balancing item is calculated to ensure that reported income was all accounted for. It consists of various small allocations of the surplus, and also some discrepancies in individual unions' accounts.

As one would expect, the larger unions tended to hire staff to cope with the volume of business: expenditure per member on salaries therefore increased from £1 per head in the smaller unions to £8 per head in the largest. On the other hand expenditure on accommodation was about £2 per person for both large and small unions.

The dividends paid represented 4.4 per cent of the members' shareholdings.*

6 NI unions paid no dividend in 1986;
14 paid less than 3 per cent;
17 paid 3 per cent;
39 paid 4 per cent
18 paid 5 per cent;
3 paid 6 per cent or more.

There was no systematic variation in the rates of dividend paid by large and small unions. But unions with a high level of assets (more than £450 per head) were able to pay dividends averaging 4.9 per cent; relatively poor unions (up to £350 assets per head) had low dividends averaging 3.0 per cent. This suggests a virtuous/vicious circle: successful unions could offer a higher dividend with which to attract in even more savings; but relatively poor unions could not offer the dividend with which to encourage the investments they needed.

### Loans
The analysis of assets showed that the average Northern Ireland credit union had advanced £428,620 to members. That is the amount outstanding at the end of 1986. The amount advanced in the course of the year averaged £374,130 – comparison between the two figures suggests that the average loan was repaid over fourteen months.

The amount loaned in the year was enough to allow each member an advance of £300. In practice, of course, each member did not get one loan: a few may have taken out two or three; many did not have a loan at all in the course of the accounting year. The number of loans issued was 0.73 per member (that is, 73 loans for every hundred members); the average loan was £412. Most Northern Ireland unions were averaging between £300 per loan and £750 per loan, though these averages could conceal a wide range of different sizes within each credit union.

It is interesting, however, to see how unions in different size brackets distributed their money. Table 1.5 shows that those with more than 1,000 members had rather more available to advance than the

---

* These figures are based on the actual amounts paid in dividends as recorded in the accounts, as a percentage of shares held at the end of the year, rather than on the declared dividend rate. '3 per cent' means 'between 3.00 and 3.99 per cent'.

smaller unions. But instead of offering their members larger sums, they actually made smaller loans, thus enabling more people to take advantage of their service.

**Table 1.5    Loans advanced by Northern Ireland credit unions, by number of members**

| Number of members | Less than 1000 | 1000 to 1999 | 2000 or more |
|---|---|---|---|
| Average amount advanced per *member* | £250 | £290 | £340 |
| Loans per member | 0.48 | 0.63 | 0.92 |
| Average per *loan* | £520 | £460 | £370 |
| (No. of unions) | (64) | (22) | (13) |

Thus the smallest unions were offering relatively few loans – perhaps because of the administrative costs of advancing and collecting them. Northern Ireland credit unions with less than 500 members averaged only 160 loans per year. The larger unions were offering more loans, often for smaller amounts: those with more than 2,000 members averaged 3,910 transactions per year – twice as many every month as the smaller unions' annual total.

The standard rate of interest on loans is 1 per cent per month, which comes to 12.7 per cent per annum compound. The income from interest on loans was 11.8 per cent of the loans due from members at the end of the year. But if the rate of return is adjusted for the change in the amount outstanding in the course of the year, it comes to 12.7 per cent, and it appears that credit unions in Northern Ireland were fully successful in obtaining their intended rate of interest.

**Institutions in Great Britain**
The first credit union in Great Britain was established in a London suburb in 1964. The numbers grew to 27 in 1974 and 40 in 1977 with a total membership of about 7,500. They had already attracted official interest. The Crowther Committee on consumer credit (1971)[1] recognised the difficulties faced by people without bank accounts in

obtaining credit at reasonable rates. And it saw the potential of credit unions for filling this gap:

> There is a prima facie case for encouraging the credit union movement and for taking steps to make its existence, its aims and methods widely known in the hope that it may take root here and more credit unions may be formed in Britain.

But before 1979, the legal framework gave credit unions three options, all of which presented obstacles to their development. First, they could register with the Registrar of Friendly Societies under the Industrial and Provident Societies Act. This was designed to regulate small cooperative ventures, but it prohibited lending except on 'the security of real or personal property'. Its effect was to silt up lending channels. Members were unable to borrow above the level of their own savings, unless another member could be found to guarantee the loan on the security of his or her savings. The level of lending was limited by the number of guarantors who were prepared both to put their own savings at risk and to forego the opportunity to take out a loan themselves.

Second, credit unions could set up as a limited company. This imposed few controls to ensure that members' savings were properly administered, but a union had to have permanent officials who would be liable for the debt of the company. The registration fees were large in relation to the turnover of these cooperative ventures. None of these requirements were compatible with a voluntary organisation.

A third option was for a credit union to remain unincorporated. This left it in a legal limbo, unable to sue or be sued. Lack of any safeguards or supervision did little to promote confidence among potential members.

The Credit Union Act was introduced in 1979. It followed the pattern set in Northern Ireland by regulating the size of loans and shareholdings, the rate of interest payable on loans and the dividend payable on shares. No member could hold more than £2,000 in shares. The maximum dividend was set at 8 per cent. No more than 1 per cent per month could be charged in interest on loans. A credit union could ask for 60 days notice before shares could be withdrawn.

A group could no longer call itself a credit union nor operate as one unless it was registered with the Registry of Friendly Societies. Qualifying for registration involved demonstrating an appropriate common bond, the usual objects of a credit union and a set of acceptable rules. The Registry was empowered to monitor credit unions by requiring an annual return from each. It could appoint an inspector to investigate the affairs of a credit union or suspend it from accepting savings or making loans. It could cancel a credit union's registration or wind it up by court order.

The underlying aim of the legislation was to protect the interests of the individual consumer – the saver and the borrower. The Registry has placed an increasing emphasis on the nature and viability of the common bond and its own powers to monitor and intervene in groups which appear to be falling short of required standards. It shares with the credit union national organisations an interest in protecting members, but it does not directly sponsor their development.

By the end of 1980, 57 credit unions had registered under the Act. Most were existing credit unions but a few, particularly among the West Indian population, had previously been more informal extended family groups who had clubbed together to save and to give each other loans. These informal loan clubs became illegal under the Act, and they were obliged to organise around an acceptable common bond such as a local club or a postal district.

A further 24 had registered by 1982. But expansion still fell short of the hopes of those who had supported the legislation. Difficulties began to appear. The redefinition of common bonds for initial registration had led to the creation of wide membership fields (for instance the use of postal districts in the London area). The large number of people in these areas did not necessarily feel a strong 'actual' common bond, and this led to increased risks of default on debts. Smaller credit unions now found it a burden to pay the registration fees and this prevented many of them from offering dividends to their members. The need to produce an annual return and the requirement for a professional audit caused problems for smaller community based groups. It was often difficult for the volunteer managers to upgrade their standards to a professional level.

During 1982 the Registry began to investigate inadequate administration and accounting systems in some credit unions who had submitted annual returns late or badly completed. It reported:

> Some credit unions were formed and registered in a spirit of optimism engendered by the provision of a specific statutory framework. Inevitably, in some cases, the euphoria present at the launching of a new enterprise has given way to the more sober realisation that the day-to-day responsibility of running the

enterprise effectively and prudently involves a great deal of commitment and voluntary effort by individuals. Regrettably, not all of those involved had appreciated the scope and depth of their responsibilities to take care of the funds their members placed with them, or the time necessary to discharge them adequately[2].

Between 1983 and 1985, only seven credit unions were started, and six were closed. These difficulties led the Registry to impose some new requirements on credit unions. In particular:

- The completion of a quarterly return (in addition to the annual return) to provide an early warning system for credit unions in difficulties.

- A requirement to provide sufficient information prior to registration to satisfy the Registrar of an adequate basic management capability and a system of control. This was to include assurances as to elected officers' access to training and the likelihood of successors to the present office-holders being found if necessary.

The Registry was also concerned to establish the 'reality' of the proposed common bond:

Some common bonds, while qualifying in a technical sense, lacked the real community of interest which lies or should lie at the heart of the common bond if it is to fulfil one of its main functions of reducing the risk of financial failure or management collapse[3].

In deciding the adequacy of common bonds, the Registry now considers: the cohesiveness of its membership and the extent to which one member is known to the others; the sense of commitment or obligation of the members; the frequency of contact between members; the ability of a member in difficulty with repaying a loan to opt out or walk away; the existence of backing from an employer; the geographical spread of the organisation and the expected significance of the credit union to the organisation or community from which its members are drawn. But the critical test for registration remains whether:

the particular features of the proposed union (are) such that there is a reasonable expectation that it will be able and willing to safeguard properly the money of members placed with it[4].

After the pause in growth between 1982 and 1985, there has been a big increase in the number of credit unions: from 82 at the end of 1985 to 94 in 1986, and a 108 in 1987. Membership had reached

27,000 by the end of 1987. The Registry reports that another 41 unions had been formed by November 1988. But seven older unions had failed during the year. The number of unions at the most recent count was therefore 142 – a growth of 72 per cent over three years. The number of members must have reached about 35,000 by the end of 1988.

Credit unions in Great Britain have to choose which of two umbrella groups they should join. The Association of British Credit Unions (ABCUL, previously the Credit Union League) represents 109 credit unions in England, Scotland and Wales. ABCUL, which is the direct equivalent of the Irish League, is affiliated to the World Council of Credit Unions, backed by the major American association. ABCUL employs ten staff, and its head office has recently been transferred from Lancashire to London. It currently receives a grant of about £260,000 per year from the World Council. In addition local authorities support three of its development workers.

The National Federation of Credit Unions is the smaller group. Until 1986 it had only ten members in Great Britain, plus two recent recruits in Northern Ireland. But the Federation has been successful during the recent expansion in credit union numbers, and now has 27 British members. Its headquarters in Bradford are supported in part by a grant from the local council to cover development work in the area.

The rival organisations trace their histories back to founders who took different positions in the debate between the *instrumental* and the *idealistic* approaches to credit unions, and they retain these differences in emphasis. The Association (ABCUL) favours the *instrumental* view, and focusses on structures, organisation and growth. The Federation (NFCU) takes a more *idealistic* line, and concentrates on community development, self-help and small units.

These differences in philosophy lead to three differences in practice. First, in the organisational structure of individual credit unions. ABCUL member-unions adopt a standard constitution involving a Board of Directors in charge of policy, a Loans Committee responsible for assessing credit applications, and a small Supervisory Committee to ensure that the other two bodies keep within the rules. NFCU member-unions, in contrast, have a single Committee responsible for all aspects of the the credit union's operation. It can be seen that the first style may be overelaborate for a very small credit union, while the second may be insufficiently sophisticated for a very large one.

The second difference between the two groups is in their perception of the role of a national organisation. The National Federation provides a meeting point for its members, a voice in national debates, and support for community groups thinking of setting up a union. This is a low profile organisation, in keeping with the idealistic preference for grass-roots over hierarchy. The Association, in contrast, sees itself as the arm of a worldwide movement aiming to promote the credit union ideal in this country. As well as providing services to members and candidates it actively develops new credit unions through field staff and has established standard systems and training procedures. On a regional level it organises Chapters to facilitate training and the exchange of experiences between union officers. And it has a policing function, with a programme of regular monitoring and inspections to ensure that member-unions meet the legal requirements.

The third important difference between the members of the two organisations is in their view of growth. The Association sees it as important that existing credit unions should build up their membership and their assets to reach a sounder financial footing and take a larger share of the savings and credit market. And it wants to expand the number of new credit unions, not only in order to bring the benefits of membership to a wider population, but also to strengthen the movement as a whole. The aim is to build up a self-sufficient movement, independent of American resources. In view of the difficulties experienced by small credit unions in the early 1980s, and the drain on the Association's own funds, it decided to

> focus resources on those results that create the greatest contribution to its own financial independence and self-sufficiency[5].

In practice, this *instrumental* approach meant emphasising large workplace based credit unions in preference to smaller groups in residential communities.

For some years the Association took what many members of the movement considered to be an extreme position on this issue. In the last year or two, however, it has adopted a broader strategy, recognising the need for growth, but not at the expense of existing small community credit unions or newly developing community groups.

The members of the Federation, in contrast, have placed more emphasis on meeting the needs of people suffering economic disadvantage, and see the value of credit unions at least as much in terms of self-help and community development as in providing financial services. The Federation prefers credit unions not to exceed a few hundred members, in order to retain their voluntary style of management and close contact with the membership. Expansion ought to concentrate on the development of new small unions in more communities, rather than on the growth of existing groups. The benefits of voluntary action in fostering the self-help ethos, empowerment and personal development of the individual are seen to outweigh those of increasing business efficiency and the economies of scale which would come from a larger, professionally run organisation.

If the aim of legislation is to protect the individual consumer, then the objectives of umbrella organisations have been to develop and support a self-sufficient, autonomous credit union movement capable of supervising its own membership and providing for all its needs. Yet the strength of the national credit union organisation has a bearing on the extent to which the Registry performs policing and monitoring functions. In Ireland the success of the movement as a whole has fostered the development of a strong and well-resourced League, and the public authorities on both sides of the border have assigned much of the responsibility for routine monitoring to the representative organisation. In Great Britain, on the other hand, under-resourced and split national organisations have not been able to provide sufficient support to affiliated credit unions in difficulties. The Registrar has therefore been much more directly involved in the supervision of individual unions.

In some parts of the country the credit union umbrella groups and/or local authorities have employed development workers to promote and assist credit unions in the area. Many of these initiatives rely on short-term grant aid, and the pattern is therefore subject to fluctuation. There were thirteen at the beginning of 1988, and proposals for several more posts have been put forward in the course of the year.

These development posts have often been set up in partnership between local authorities and the representatives of the existing credit union movement. But they have set up tensions which reflect some of the problems in the American movement described in the Introduction. Credit unions have an appeal to local authorities which spans the political spectrum: to notions of thrift and self-help and to a desire for increasing citizen participation and empowerment. Development workers have often been appointed as part of an authority's anti-poverty strategy, as a means of alleviating the financial hardship and debt problems of low income families. It has also been hoped that credit unions would improve the economic infrastructure, decreasing the outflow of money from local areas and offering support to small businesses. Hence most development workers are expected to concentrate their time and expertise on setting up credit unions, particularly community based credit unions, in areas of greatest need.

This focus on disadvantaged areas contrasts with the broader strategy of also developing more commercially attractive, workplace based credit unions. As far as ABCUL is concerned the latter are essential to a viable and self-sufficient movement and to a well-resourced national organisation. There has also been dispute about development workers' setting up new credit unions rather than supporting those already in existence. Credit unions not only need help during the starting up process but also continuing technical assistance during their first few years, until they can achieve stability and financial self-sufficiency. It is feared that overenthusiastic development may create a short-lived blossoming of unions in areas where they cannot survive without a disproportionate input of resources and support. There might be serious consequences for already under-resourced national organisations and for the general reputation of credit unions. These arguments can put development workers employed by the Association with local authority funding in a difficult position.

Although credit unions have been set up in most parts of Great Britain, there are few or none in the purely rural regions – the South West of England or East Anglia (Table 1.6). The largest concentrations are in the South East and Scotland. Within each region, the great majority of British credit unions are in urban areas such as London, Birmingham, the Northern conurbations, or Glasgow and its surrounding towns. Credit unions share this urban concentration with many other types of community initiative; but the same is not true of Northern Ireland, where more than three-quarters of the unions and of their members are outside the two principal centres of population.

**Table 1.6    Regional distribution of credit unions in Great Britain, 1986**

|  | Number of of unions | Number of members | Percentage of adult population |
|---|---|---|---|
| Scotland | 15 | 6330 | 0.15 |
| North | 3 | 430 | 0.02 |
| North-west | 7 | 2960 | 0.06 |
| Yorks and Humberside | 9 | 1170 | 0.03 |
| West Midlands | 5 | 360 | 0.01 |
| East Midlands | 7 | 630 | 0.02 |
| East Anglia | nil | nil | nil |
| Wales | 1 | 310 | 0.01 |
| South west | 1 | 450 | 0.01 |
| South east | 27 | 8640 | 0.06 |

Note:    Table based on the 75 unions for which full details were recorded.

The more striking contrast with Northern Ireland, though, is the relative scarcity of credit unions in all parts of Great Britain. In no region does membership approach one per cent of adults. Members of the Catholic population of Northern Ireland are more than 300 times more likely to belong to a credit union than people in mainland Britain.

Of the 108 British credit unions in existence at the end of 1987:

- 42 formed their common bond among the residents of a particular area; some of these areas are based on church parish boundaries and the common bond is therefore not purely geographical;
- 29 had a common bond based on membership of a 'bona fide organisation'. We estimate that about half of these were based on a church or group of churches; the majority but not all of these Christian credit unions were Catholic;
- 19 had a dual common bond: members could *either* live in a particular area *or* belong to a particular organisation;
- 16 restricted membership to those who work for a particular employer; a relatively high proportion of these workplace credit unions were based on a local authority, where council members have sometimes supported the development of cooperative schemes of this sort.

• The final 2 unions based their common bond on membership of a particular occupation and employment in a particular area respectively.

This variety of common bonds also contrasts with Northern Ireland, where almost all credit unions have an official common bond defined in terms of a particular area, and most have an unofficial link with the Catholic Church.

## Financial structure in Great Britain
### *Members*
Analysis of the 1986 returns for the 75 established credit unions in Great Britain shows that the average British union was a quarter the size of its Northern Ireland counterpart: 280 members compared with 1240:

21 credit unions in Great Britain had less than 100 members;
27 had between 100 and 199;
11 had between 200 and 299;
8 had between 300 and 499;
12 had 500 members or more.

So the great majority of British unions would be considered small by Northern Irish standards: three-quarters of British unions had fewer than 300 members; only one twelfth of Northern Irish unions were as small as that.

Workplace-based credit unions tended to be relatively large, averaging 570 members; where the common bond was based on a (non-religious) association, membership tended to be low, averaging 140. The average membership of National Federation credit unions was only two-thirds as large as for unions affiliated to the Association, and this accords with the declared preferences of the two organisations which have already been discussed.

British credit unions experienced slightly higher rates both of membership turnover and of growth than were seen in Northern Ireland in recent years. The average union of 280 members reported that about 32 members left each year, but about 60 joined. The typical credit union grew by about 60 per cent between 1981 and 1986.

## Assets

British credit unions had an average of £72,260 in assets; £260 per member (Table 1.7). Unions in Great Britain were therefore much poorer than those in Northern Ireland, mainly because they had fewer members, but also partly because of lower assets per member. Three-quarters of British unions had less than £250 per member; hardly any Northern Irish unions (1 out of 20) were as poor as that.

**Table 1.7   Assets of credit unions in Great Britain**

|  | Average per union | Percent of total | Compare N.I. |
|---|---|---|---|
| **Assets** | | | |
| Loans to members | £62,870 | 87% | (80%) |
| less accumulated provision for bad and doubtful debts | (£1,610) | (2%) | ((2%)) |
| Investments | £1,750 | 2% | (8%) |
| Cash | £6,930 | 10% | (7%) |
| Fixed assets | £1,750 | 2% | (6%) |
| Prepayments | £150 | * | (1%) |
| Sundry debtors | £420 | 1% | (1%) |
| TOTAL | £72,260 | 100% | (100%) |
| **Represented by** | | | |
| Share capital | £61,760 | 85% | (85%) |
| Juvenile deposits | £280 | * | na |
| General reserve | £3,720 | 5% | (9%) |
| Other reserves | £820 | 1% | na |
| Unappropriated surplus carried forward | £590 | 1% | (*) |
| Dividends payable | £1,800 | 2% | (4%) |
| Creditors and charges | £980 | 1% | (1%) |
| Provision for taxation | £160 | * | (*) |
| Loans and interest | £440 | 1% | (*) |
| Balancing item[+] | £1,710 | 2% | (1%) |
| TOTAL | £72,260 | 100% | (100%) |

* = less than 0.5%
[+] The balancing item is calculated to ensure that reported assets are all accounted for. It consists of various small items, plus discrepancies in individual unions' accounts.

Fifteen credit unions in Great Britain had less than £100 per member, and their viability must be in doubt.

Although British unions were poorer than their Northern Irish counterparts, their financial base was expanding. The 54 unions which returned figures for the complete sequence of years from 1982 to 1986 increased their assets per member from £160 to £260 over that period, at 1986 prices. The rate of growth of was about 13 per cent per year, during a period when the real level of assets per member in Northern Ireland remained stable.

The structure of credit unions' finances was similar on both sides of the water, with the great majority of assets consisting of members' shares, most of it loaned back out to members. But British unions had relatively low levels of investment in outside institutions, and few fixed assets. In contrast, they held relatively high stocks of cash. The level of British unions' reserves ought to cause some concern, given the Credit Union Act's target of 10 per cent of assets. Half of them had a general reserve representing less than 4 per cent of their total assets.

In Northern Ireland, the analysis of assets did not show very consistent differences between the large and (relatively) small groups. In Great Britain, on the other hand, the smallest credit unions operated

**Table 1.8   Assets of British credit unions, by number of members**

| Number of members | Less than 100 | 100 to 199 | 200 to 299 | 300 to 499 | 500 or more |
|---|---|---|---|---|---|
| Mean assets per member | £130 | £160 | £240 | £310 | £290 |
| *Principal items as percentage of total* | | | | | |
| Due from members | 77% | 71% | 78% | 82% | 93% |
| Investments | * | 4% | nil | 10% | * |
| Cash | 24% | 21% | 17% | 9% | 6% |
| Fixed assets | * | * | 8% | * | 2% |
| Share capital | 88% | 86% | 86% | 83% | 88% |
| General reserve | 5% | 4% | 4% | 9% | 5% |
| (No. of unions) | (21) | (22) | (11) | (8) | (12) |

* = less than 0.5%

on a significantly narrower financial base than the (relatively) large ones (Table 1.8). Those with less than 200 members had only £150 per person, compared with £275 per person where there were more than 200 members. More detailed analysis (not shown in the table) suggests that those unions which increased the number of their members over the last five years reported about twice the level of assets per head of unions with stable or declining memberships.

The smaller the union, the larger the proportion of all assets which were locked up in cash, and this left the small unions even more short of funds available for loans or other applications. More than half of the smallest British unions reported reserves of less than 2 per cent of their assets, and this must leave them in a risky position.

There were also variations according to the nature of the common bond: unions based on workplaces or on churches were relatively wealthy, averaging £340 per member; those based on residence or (non-church) associations averaged £160 – less than half as much.

### Income and expenditure

The income of a credit union is almost entirely derived from its assets, and the pattern of revenue in Great Britain closely follows the analysis of capital in the preceding paragraphs (Table 1.9). The overall average annual income of £27 per member ranged from £32 in the larger groups to only £15 in the smaller groups.

**Table 1.9    Income of credit unions in Great Britain**

|  | Average per union | Percent of total | Compare N.I. |
|---|---|---|---|
| **Income** | | | |
| Interest from loans to members | £6,310 | 85% | (84%) |
| Investment interest | £220 | 3% | (7%) |
| Bank interest | £280 | 4% | (4%) |
| Bad debts recovered | £30 | * | (2%) |
| Other income | £610 | 8% | (2%) |
| TOTAL | £7,450 | 100% | 100% |

* = less than 0.5%

**Table 1.10  Expenditure of credit unions in Great Britain**

| | Average per union | Percent of total income | Compare N.I. |
|---|---|---|---|
| **Expenditure** | | | |
| Salaries | £410 | 6% | (13%) |
| Loan insurance | £640 | 9% | (7%) |
| Accommodation | £200 | 3% | (5%) |
| Postage, printing, travel etc | £150 | 2% | (3%) |
| Audit charges | £430 | 6% | (2%) |
| Other management expenses | £1,140 | 15% | (4%) |
| Total management expenses | £2,970 | 40% | (34%) |
| Provision for bad and doubtful debts | £570 | 8% | (11%) |
| Taxation | £160 | 2% | (3%) |
| Depreciation | £120 | 2% | (3%) |
| Other outgoings | £410 | 6% | (1%) |
| TOTAL EXPENDITURE | £4,230 | 57% | (52%) |
| **Application of surplus** | | | |
| Dividend on shares | £2,190 | 29% | (33%) |
| Rebate of loan interest | £60 | 1% | (1%) |
| Transfer to reserve (net) | £450 | 6% | (12%) |
| Balancing item[+] | £520 | 7% | (2%) |
| TOTAL SURPLUS | £3,220 | 43% | (48%) |
| TOTAL INCOME | £7,450 | 100% | (100%) |

[+] The balancing item is calculated to ensure that all reported income is accounted for. It consists of various small allocations of the surplus, and also some discrepancies in individual unions' accounts.

The accounts demanded by the Registrars in London and Belfast record expenditure under somewhat different headings, and it is not possible to make exactly reliable comparisons between the two sets of figures. In Great Britain, in particular, a total of 28 per cent of income was attributed to various non-specific categories of expenditure*, compared with only 7 per cent in Northern Ireland (Table 1.10).

---

* 'Other management expenses', 'other outgoings' and 'balancing item'.

It can be seen that British unions spent relatively small proportions of their scarce resources on salaries and accommodation; their smaller size allowed most of them to operate without staff and fixed offices.

In spite of lower costs on these activities, British credit unions had to allocate a lower proportion of their income to a dividend, and to general reserves, than their Northern Ireland counterparts could afford. It was found in Northern Ireland that richer unions were able to pay higher dividends than those with lower levels of assets. In Great Britain, dividends were very strongly related both to the size of the union, and to its financial standing. While most of the larger and richer British unions were able to pay a dividend in line with the Northern Ireland rate, few of the smaller and poorer groups could pay any dividend at all (Table 1.11).

**Table 1.11  Dividend on shares in Great Britain, by number of members and by assets per head**

| Number of members | Less than 100 | 100 to 149 | 150 to 299 | 300 more |
|---|---|---|---|---|
| Proportion paying any dividend | 38% | 60% | 72% | 85% |
| Average dividend (if paid) | 6.3% | 3.3% | 4.3% | 4.8% |
| (No. of unions) | (21) | (15) | (18) | (20) |
| **Assets per head** | Less than £100 | £100 to £149 | £150 to £199 | £200 or more |
| Proportion paying any dividend | 20% | 65% | 69% | 91% |
| Average dividend (if paid) | 2.5% | 2.5% | 3.6% | 4.7% |
| (No. of unions) | (15) | (20) | (16) | (22) |

Note:    Figures based on the actual amounts recorded as dividends in the annual accounts, as a percentage of shares held at the end of the year, rather than the declared dividend rate.

## *Loans*

The average British credit union had loans outstanding to members amounting to about £63,000 – about £220 per member. Another way of recording loans is the amount advanced in the course of the year: the average in Great Britain was £72,340. In other words, British unions were loaning out each available pound a bit more often than once a year, and this rapid turnover would stretch the scarce resources further than in Northern Ireland, where it took rather more than a year before a pound could be relent. This means, of course, that British members were expected to repay their loans in a shorter period – 10 months, on average, compared with 14 months in Northern Ireland.

Even at the accelerated turnover, British credit unions had less to loan than their equivalents in Ulster. They might respond either by making fewer loans (in relation to the size of their membership), or by loaning smaller amounts on each occasion. In practice, they tend to have chosen the former. The size of loans advanced in the two sectors was remarkably similar, as Table 1.12 shows. But members in Britain were rather less likely to obtain a loan than those in Northern Ireland.

In Northern Ireland, it was found that larger and/or richer credit unions tended to use their funds to increase the number of loans available, rather than to increase their size. In Great Britain, the

**Table 1.12  Distribution of loans to members: Great Britain and Northern Ireland compared**

|  | Northern Ireland | Great Britain |
|---|---|---|
| Loan capital per member | £345 | £219 |
| Amount advanced in year, per £ of capital available | 0.87 | 1.17 |
| Loans per member | 0.72 | 0.61 |
| Average amount per loan | £416 | £419 |
| Size of loans: |  |  |
| £1 - £250 | 54% | 54% |
| £251 - £500 | 24% | 26% |
| £501 - £1,000 | 14% | 13% |
| £1,001 - £2,000 | 7% | 6% |
| More than £2,000 | 1% | 2% |

**Table 1.13   Loans advanced by credit unions in Great Britain, by number of members**

| Number of members | Less than 100 | 100 to 199 | 200 to 299 | 300 to 499 | 500 or more |
|---|---|---|---|---|---|
| Average amount advanced per *member* | £120 | £150 | £170 | £290 | £310 |
| Loans per member | 0.55 | 0.54 | 0.45 | 0.72 | 0.65 |
| Average per *loan* | £220 | £280 | £370 | £400 | £480 |
| (No. of unions) | (21) | (22) | (11) | (8) | (12) |

analysis shows the opposite: bigger and richer unions tended to offer roughly similar numbers of loans to their members, but advanced larger amounts (Table 1.13).

Thus although the overall pattern of loans shown in Table 1.12 was broadly similar, Britain and Northern Ireland were rather different in detail. Another difference was in the degree of consistency. In Northern Ireland, well over half of all unions reported an average per loan within the range £400 to £750; none advanced less than £200 per loan on average; none advanced more than £1,000 on average. In Great Britain, in contrast, there was a much wider range of policies: less than a quarter lay in the range £400 to £750; 14 unions averaged less than £200 per loan; and three averaged more than £1,000 a time.

Interest charged at 1 per cent per month ought to yield 12.7 per cent per year. But a few British unions charge only 9 per cent. In Northern Ireland the income from interest payments exactly equalled 12.7 per cent of the loan fund (averaged over the year). The equivalent calculation in Great Britain showed that income from interest averaged 11.0 per cent of loans.

### References

1. Crowther Committee, *Report of the committee on consumer credit.* HMSO, 1971.
2. *Report of the Registrar of Friendly Societies*, 1981/82, HMSO.
3. *Report of the Registrar of Friendly Societies*, 1982/83, HMSO.
4. Registry of Friendly Societies, *Note for the Guidance of Applicants*, April 1986.
5. Credit Union League of Great Britain, *Annual report*, 1981.

# 2. Running a Credit Union

This chapter looks at credit unions from the point of view of the people responsible for setting them up and managing them. Most of the material draws on the experience of the twelve unions chosen for more detailed study, and that of development workers employed by the national organisations or local authorities.

## Getting started

Although various organisations are keen to promote new credit unions, it is recognised that the initiative should come from the grass roots. Most credit unions started with the perception of a need for financial services.

> There was one particular shop that everybody (round here) had an account in and a collector called every week to collect your money. You bought your furniture, curtain material, your bedding, your clothes, your shoes, your nursery items from the one firm. And you were tied to that firm. You were committed to whatever prices they chose to charge. You didn't have the choice of being able to shop around or even buy from newspapers where people would be advertising used prams and things. You didn't have the ready money to answer an ad in the paper. It was easier to get a new thing than it was to be thrifty and buy second hand.

> The level of poverty in the Borough is appalling ... Our money advice shops experience that. In an attempt to try and reduce the number of council employees making use of those shops, they felt that the credit union would be a very practical way of helping.

> There's very little money in this community ... There's very few people with savings; there's quite a few loan sharks; there's quite a few people use the Provident. People who save with the credit

union, it brings some self respect back to them. They've got money
that belongs to them.

Typically, one or two people who had heard about credit unions
would suggest the idea to a small group who became the founder
members. The founding group were often people who themselves
were financially stable but who felt there was a need among the local
population. Among those in the sample, five had first heard about
credit unions through the Catholic church, three from people involved
in other credit unions, one from a community worker and a further
three from local government officials involved in people's financial
problems.

> A group of people got together and decided that they would start a
> credit union after listening to a talk by a priest. It was a time of
> high unemployment and they thought that the time was ripe to try
> and do something for one another.

> My husband and another fellow just got together and invited their
> immediate neighbours in the street to join. It sort of snowballed
> from that. People probably who wouldn't actually need the credit
> union started it.

> We got off the ground when the local church felt there was a need
> because of growth in the area with new housing estates. They
> asked certain people to join to start up a credit union. Eleven men
> got together and we had 15 in a short space of time. We spent
> about three months studying and saving. Then we held a public
> meeting and we enrolled about 130 people.

A usual first step was to ask one of the national organisations or a
local credit union development worker for information and advice.
Some embryo groups turned to generalist community or social
workers for advice at this stage, but the credit union specialists were
often unhappy about this. They felt that inexperienced advisers
unthinkingly assumed that 'anyone can have a credit union', without
appreciating the technical and legal problems. Their tendency to
concentrate on group dynamics rather than book-keeping was said to
have led some embryo groups into bad practices which were difficult
to correct.

When the initial information had been provided, the group was
asked to make contact again if they were still interested. The initiative
was left to the enquirers, as a check on the strength of their motivation.
There are many enquiries but few credit unions. If contact was
renewed, most development workers would visit the group to present

a slide show or video. The worker would try to assess the group's potential. As one worker said, 'I try to put them off and I usually succeed'.

The next stage was usually the formation of a steering group to discuss the aims of a credit union, its powers and limits, administration, the legislation and rules, the role of the national organisations. Potential officers would be approached and support rustled up from personal contacts and local organisations: PTAs, mothers' and toddlers' groups, ethnic organisations, the church and so on.

The most important question facing a potential credit union was the nature and strength of the common bond. A bond could not be created; it had to exist. Credit unions might flourish in strong communities, but in many areas – perhaps especially in disadvantaged areas – 'the community' and 'poverty' were concepts too loose to provide any real links between the prospective members of a credit union. Many credit unions have been set up by local churches, but several of those in our sample suggested that their success had been based on the loyalty of existing church-goers rather than on recruitment among a wider public.

Credit unions must have 22 sponsors to sign the registration form and (more recently) to pledge two years' support to the group. The sponsors should include people capable of running the credit union, and in particular to keep the accounts: a treasurer, two assistants and a cashier, estimated at 30 hours of work per week between them. If no-one with experience of these activities was available, training of volunteers was essential right at the start.

> You may not have anybody among a group of people who has any formal training in that sort of area. Whilst theoretically it's very straightforward, in practice it's not that easy. It's having someone with the necessary expertise who happens to be on the committee who can handle that sort of thing. If you don't then you need to train someone to do it, otherwise the whole thing falls down.

Most embryo credit unions worked out a business plan to establish policies on shares and loans, interest and dividend rates, entrance fees, insurance, reserves and credit control. An auditor had to be appointed.

The union could then request registration. Until recently, there were often administrative obstacles outside the control of the embryo union. Groups sponsored by ABCUL were having their application held up by short-staffing at headquarters. Further delays could follow in negotiating with the Registry, so that it might take three or four months for queries to be raised and dealt with. Such delays, at a time when many groups were fully prepared with an expectant membership, could bring both officers and members 'off the boil' and undermine their morale. Both ABCUL and the Registry have, however, assured us that registrations can now be achieved much more rapidly.

It is not clear whether the law allows credit unions to pool the savings of members before they have been formally registered. ABCUL has adopted a cautious approach, but the National Federation promotes savings clubs as a stage in the development of credit unions. Without savings, it was difficult to find the registration fee and purchase equipment, unless a grant could be obtained. Pre-savings could also speed the build-up of capital to the point at which loans could be offered.

Development workers suggested that it might take between six months and three years to set up a credit union, depending on the characteristics of the group, the nature of the common bond, and the Registrar's initial response to the application. Occupational credit unions were often the quickest to get off the ground, because of the existing chain of command, the availability of administrative skills and, often, the support of the employer. With community based unions it was often difficult to build up a confident working group, especially if the members had low levels of education and lacked experience of administration and negotiation. An assumption that 'everything would be done for them' could hinder the acceptance of personal responsibility for the affairs of the credit union. Supporting the management group without taking over its duties could occupy much of a development worker's time, both before and after registration.

## The leadership group
Credit unions belong to their members, and are administered by elected officers: the three-way structure of Board, Credit Committee and Supervisory Committee required by the Irish League and British Association, or the single Committee recommended by the National Federation. The credit unions examined in depth had elected between seven and fifteen volunteers to the Board or Management Committee, according to the overall size of their total membership.

Credit committees consisted of three to seven members, usually meeting weekly. Four credit unions had also authorised a loans officer to grant loans without reference to the committee, within certain limits. Supervisory committees had three members, meeting from time to time to carry out spot checks on operations and at collections.

As well as the normal range of officers, most unions had also selected one or two assistant treasurers, and in some cases specialist officers or committees to deal with particular aspects of the operation – education and membership officers, insurance officers, credit control officers. One credit union had a committee to oversee its premises. Sometimes an ad hoc committee would be asked to organise a social evening.

All but two of the credit unions under study called for volunteers from the general membership to help. In some cases volunteers were organised into a rota of collectors, tellers or cashiers. Ordinary members were also involved in making tea or food, and in explaining the ropes to new members. And several officers said they could draw on individual members' expertise on such subjects as law or accountancy.

The success of a credit union (like any voluntary group) depends on the services of a committed group of elected officers. Many of the leaders were motivated by a commitment to helping others and a belief in the philosophy of the credit union movement:

> I don't think there's many officers who join the credit union because they can get a loan at a cheaper rate. There has to be a social conscience to become an officer. I think it's a social conscience that most people need to give up time. It's an opportunity for me to do something in the community where I live.

> It does give you satisfaction especially when you get people coming in who are in trouble and you can help them. It's so easy to help them, there's nobody else to turn to, only the credit union. It's a last resort.

> I got interested by the fact I was involved in trade unions, also in the labour movement which is a social movement. We made many demands for things and many services over the years which weren't met. When we learned about credit unions we realised what it could provide.

But there was also a combination of self-interested and altruistic motives:

You're helping yourself to help other people. With being a member yourself the money is there for you to borrow as well as for everybody else to borrow.

I feel that if I didn't do my bit to assist, the thing might just collapse and it would be of disbenefit to me, because I'm still keen on borrowing money cheaply.

## The social contacts were also appreciated:

You get to know a lot of people. I didn't know anybody up here and I know a lot of people now. I'd been 16 years here and I didn't know ten people. But I really enjoy it.

My interest, it wasn't motivated by any high ideals at all. I was a young mother with a large family and a low income and very little social life, very little social contact outside my own home. It was a cheap way of socialising for me in the beginning. It went on from there. I got a taste for it.

There's a great social aspect to it right throughout the country for the whole spread of the movement, the credit union gospel. You meet people from all over the country where they're doing the very same thing that you're doing. It refuels you and gives you the heart to go on.

## Many said that they got satisfaction out of knowing that the union was running well and out of the interest and challenge involved in the work.

I really got interested in it all right. I could see it was doing some good in the community. It was a challenge too, whatever ability you had. There's a certain amount of money there, and there's some people who want it. What did you know about them? What were the prospects of those people paying you back if you lent them a certain amount of money? It got very interesting and it was a great challenge.

The satisfaction was there when I did my first financial report and I managed it. For each financial report there is a small satisfaction. If we solve some delinquencies there is a big satisfaction there.

## And people had gained personally from the experience of running the credit union, acquiring skills and broadening their outlook on life:

You learn a lot by the jobs you do. I have, through being Secretary. Things like how to write letters properly, even typing – I could never type like I do now ... Different things that I never thought I could do.

People have said when they've gone on from here to jobs they've applied for on the strength of their credit union experience and got them. We're always having to give references out.

> I think maybe particularly women would agree that we've all developed as individuals ... When you're raising a family you become very reticent and your conversation is in a very limited area because you're dealing with kids all the time. You lose confidence and everything else and I think every one of us has discovered that we've got talents that were there all the time but that weren't used before. We've got voices now that we would never have had. We would never have stood up in front of a crowd of people and spoken before. Now we do and it doesn't really bother us all that much. It develops your character as well and all the latent gifts come out of people.

But there was also a fear of failure:

> The big disadvantage is taking on all this work and finding that it's failed. We're terrified of that I would say, all of us.

And, although there was a great deal to be gained from being a credit union officer, there were also sacrifices. Many felt the satisfactions outweighed the costs, but some pointed out the disadvantages. The time involved had had its effects on family life:

> I've been asked by my husband time and time again, am I married to the credit union? But I suppose once you start giving up your time and you see and know the benefit of the credit union you never worry about it much.

> The workload does put quite a few people off. The fewer you've got the more arduous it does obviously get. I've had quite a few people, who quite like the idea of a credit union, shy away from it because it sounds as if there's just too much work involved. I wish there was some way of lessening that.

> There are times when you can't get far enough away from the credit union. When you come in, especially in the winter, just to sit down and have your tea and watch the television.

Although the majority of officers said that they had to spend no more than three hours per week on credit union business, others put in much more time – up to 20 hours each week. The most time-consuming roles were Treasurer and President. Those working hardest for the credit union were often the people who had heavy commitments elsewhere. As one long-serving officer remarked: 'It's the old adage, ask a person who's too busy to do anything and they'll do it.' For instance, eight of the ten officers who put in more than six hours a week for the credit union also had full-time jobs. Over half of those interviewed also spent time helping to organise other groups in the community: scouts or guides, church groups, trade unions, tenants' associations, and various charitable organisations. Three were school governors and two sat on the local community council.

Of the 63 officers who provided details of their experience, 16 said they had not received any training for their position with the credit union. As one chairwoman said, 'You sort of educate yourself and you can pass these skills onto other people'. A further 35 said that they had been trained by other officers, but 12 had attended training sessions organised outside their own credit union, usually by the umbrella organisations or development workers. Most however agreed that, as well as the skills they had brought with them, most of what they knew thay had learned through experience on the job.

The leadership group was not, of course, a straight cross-section of the membership. To a certain extent, committee members and other helpers tended to be the middle-aged, middle-class males who are so often found to have gravitated to positions of power and responsibility in all sorts of organisations. Analysis of the 'leaders' (committee members and other helpers) identified in our survey of members of seven credit unions showed that:

- 60 per cent of the leaders were between the ages of 40 and 65, compared with 33 per cent of the non-leaders;
- 40 per cent of the leaders were in the professional or managerial occupational group, compared with 14 per cent of the non-leaders;
- 67 per cent of the leaders were men, compared with 42 per cent of the non-leaders.

Thus the leadership's need for people with experience of administration and accountancy has led members of socially dominant groups into positions of influence within credit unions. Nevertheless (as some of the examples quoted in the last two pages illustrated) there were still opportunities and challenges for people, such as working class women, who were not 'typical' leaders. And it will be seen in the next chapter that most members felt content to save and borrow without any direct involvement in the affairs of the union.

It was striking that almost 60 per cent of the officers who filled out self-completion questionnaires had served for longer than four years. Indeed, a third had been involved in running the credit union for ten years or more; in one case for 25 years. As one officer said, 'It's just become a way of life; it's part of my life'.

The problem, in fact, lay in persuading new people to join the leadership. A credit union could become over-dependent on an established group of leaders, who might get stuck with their roles. The ideal was a combination of experienced members and new faces.

> We need people who haven't become disillusioned with the movement to help (give it) a push. It's like having a blood transfusion. The existing members (of the Board) have been in, on and off, since 1971 and despite their initial drive, when you come up against problems like delinquency, it does tend to disillusion you. It's very difficult to get yourself up and say, 'Well let's try and do something about it'.

> We do need new people coming in, but at the same time we need people with experience. I think right now we're getting somewhere. We've got experienced people who know what's been going on. We've got people with drive who feel that they've got something to add.

> When you get a committee trained it's very difficult to consider chopping and changing them all at once. So we've always got to try and introduce a new person all the time. Some people pick it up quickly and others take a bit longer. It's fair to say that once you get on a committee it's difficult to walk away from it.

But finding people to take on responsibilities was not at all easy.

> You find that a lot of members are not particularly interested, with them knowing you for so long and knowing that everything has been running smoothly. They don't want to rock the boat. They sort of say, 'I know my money is alright'. They won't come themselves.

> It is difficult enough to get new blood in at this stage. I think that's probably a very natural progression. In the early days there had to be a pioneering spirit. Well the pioneering spirit has died in this organisation... It's not as exciting now as it was in the early stages.

As a result, there was general agreement that 'there's no such a thing as a true volunteer, we have to Shanghai them.'

> At the annual meeting you don't have the election type situation where you've more standing ... than you need. You usually find that it's the same people are re-elected year after year after year, because no one wants to give up their time.

> Usually what we do when we know somebody is leaving the committee, we make a shortlist of people we think would be suitable and might be likely to agree to coming on the committee. Then someone goes and sees them.

Some of the credit unions had active policies to involve the ordinary members in routine tasks, like collecting money, in order to create a pool of people who might later be candidates for more important posts.

> We're getting young people involved here, who've been involved since twelve years of age. The young people you see here with the tea, eventually we hope we're building on solid ground with these young people. They're coming up with the modern technology and things like that that we can benefit from long term.

> It's a long-term educational process, getting this thing working, bearing in mind the sort of area that we live in. I wouldn't say we were the most educated people. One thing we've got in our favour is that we're honourable people and we've got a lot of dignity.

## Support from other organisations

The ILCU, ABCUL and NFCU all provide services to affiliated credit unions: they represent their membership, set operating standards, and offer field services in advice, training and development work.

All credit unions had at some stage in their history received help in the form of advice and training. ILCU members were happy with the support that had been given:

> I believe strongly in the concept of the League. We set it up, the credit unions set it up and we use the field officer. He gives good advice which we listen to. We contact the insurance officer if we have any problems with insurance and the Chapter, as a wing of the League, we attend. I think if you are part of a movement, there must be a good relationship or else you're sitting in isolation and you become complacent.

> We don't need a lot of help from the League, but it's there if we do need help. It's good, it always has been. We do what we're asked to do and we support the League whenever possible. We do tell them off when they need it.

Members of ABCUL were more varied in their responses. Some had found the advice and training valuable, although they would have liked more:

> It's nice to know it's there. If problems did occur ... it is very comforting for me, not being a qualified accountant, to know that I just have to make a telephone call.

> ABCUL's support has been essential. But it wasn't as good as it could have been in the early days. ABCUL themselves were a relatively new organisation and were not quite so able to provide sufficient resources for all the credit unions that were members of

it. They sent some of the people here on training courses, which were very good. An organisation like ABCUL are the only people who can provide it. They produce manuals and guides and help with some publicity. That's essential.

## Others were more critical:

Where I feel a lack of any support or contact is through the ABCUL structure. As the President, and previously a member of the supervisory committee, nobody has offered me any training in either of those functions.

We've floundered on for periods of time with no officer assistance ... Just letters demanding various forms returned ... It's only in failing to make those returns that it produces any response ... more a slapped wrist rather than offers of help. We're expected to be self-sufficient with no training whatsoever. There should be more recognition of the fact that we're ... untrained, unpaid volunteers.

## One credit union took a strong line against ABCUL's go-for-growth policy:

They are looking for growth ... to make the thing viable so (the Americans) can withdraw their support. The fear of course is that community credit unions will not get a great deal of attention. All the community credit unions together don't pay enough money to run the Association. Community credit unions may have to go to the bottom of the list... They want to expand to pay for bureaucracy. Our credit union can pay for itself. We don't need bureaucracy... All we need is someone to give us insurance. They want somebody with £25,000 a year and an office. To get that they must have large memberships.

## Many credit unions commented favourably on the support received locally, either through regional organisations or Chapters, or just from neighbouring groups.

Small credit unions can help one another. We've helped quite a lot, helped them off the ground. They've come in here and we've showed them how the books are going. Basically I don't think that you need this hierarchy taking money out of the credit union.

We can borrow from other credit unions if there's a need. We do get assistance in many other ways by them sharing their experience with us at Chapter when all the credit unions meet together. There's a very definite bond with other credit unions. But I think we stand very much on our own. It's self-help, and by God we've had to do it ourselves.

The one credit union in our sample which had remained independent of all the national organisations had certainly found local help useful:

> If everybody came down with 'flu in the one week you can always get help from one of the other credit unions. They will send members up to cover for you if you like. We all use the one system of book-keeping. The same is used throughout the three groups so they can step in at any time and take over from us or we can go to theirs and know their system.

Some officers were particularly keen on the insurance schemes run by the ILCU and ABCUL.

> Loan protection and life savings are essential to both the members' peace of mind and the financial stability of the credit union. (It provides) in many cases the only form of insurance a member has, and (allows) small community credit unions to operate without the fear of major losses due to unpaid loans in the event of the death of the borrower.

Central government provides hardly any resources in direct support of credit unions. But a few local authorities, mostly in metropolitan areas, have tried to encourage them. Their most substantial contribution has been in funding development workers. Some have also given small grants to help new credit unions get off the ground. One of the credit unions in the sample had received £300 from the Priority Areas Team to cover registration fees and initial publicity costs. A second had attracted funding of £1,750 to purchase office equipment and a grant of £50 per year for three years to pay for stationery.

Another local authority initiative was a subsidy provided by the GLC to enable five credit unions to hire salaried managers. A few workplace credit unions have been set up among council employees, and some of these benefit from the support of the authority.

In Northern Ireland, credit unions have grown up with the support of the ILCU, without drawing on public funds. Such support might have been counter-productive, in any case.

> It would probably have not been a good thing to have had support from local councils. It would have tended to have polarised the way we worked. It would have been split along the sectarian divide from the beginning. Whereas with us being away from that, it's possible to break it down.

There are now sixteen workplace based credit unions in Great Britain (and only one in Northern Ireland) in private companies and in the public sector: transport workers, police forces, higher education institutions and council employees. Some have obtained full support from their employer in payroll deductions (for savings and loans), office space and equipment, time off work and subsidised administrators. Some had access to computer facilities or the internal post system. Two of the credit unions under study drew their members from among council employees. One had received a lot of support from the employer. The other had not. They were both asked to describe their relationship with the council:

> The council's been very sympathetic towards us and extremely helpful in many many ways. They've encouraged us as much as they possibly can. There's traditionally a very close link politically between manual workers and the politicians (in the majority Labour group). Most of the membership of the credit union is in the manual work force. That is, I think, the reason why they've been reluctant, when we were at our worst, to pull the plug and close us down. It was the effect it would have on a large number of manual workers. I think they will continue to give us support and they will be grateful when we can increase our membership to become self-sufficient. I think we will get that support until that happens.

> Our Director (of our department) ... saw it as a good thing and therefore something to be encouraged. As far as anybody in senior management outside our own department is concerned, those that do know anything about it seem to view it with great suspicion. The vast majority don't seem to know anything about it at all. That's partly due to the fact that we haven't publicised it and partly due to the fact that they aren't interested. As a rule we have no link or relationship with the council per se. We've never approached them on formal issues.

Some employers view a credit union as a fringe benefit which may add to the attractions of the employment package they can offer, and improve management-staff relations. Other employers have found it necessary to counsel staff in financial difficulties; indeed some employers, for example the police, have a statutory duty to provide this kind of support. A credit union has offered one way of tackling the problem.

The Catholic Church has played an important role, not only in initiating the development of credit unions, but also in providing premises and other services to aid their operation. Patronage by the church at a parish level can greatly enhance a credit union's image and assist it to retain the confidence of the general membership. Loyalty to the church can provide a strong common bond. For the church itself, credit union objectives of co-operation and combatting usury are in harmony with Christian principles. A church-based credit union might also help to revive a flagging congregation. On the other hand, a church-based union can project a denominational image, implying that credit unions are only for Catholics. It is notable that the success of credit unions in Northern Ireland is almost entirely confined to the Catholic population.

Many of the credit unions we visited had received some support from other groups or institutions in their local community. Some had the use of a community centre free or at a nominal rent, together with office equipment and storage space. Links had also been forged with local schools, voluntary organisations and retailers. One credit union reported substantial moral support from local retailers who found that customers were no longer running up debts on their accounts.

## Premises and staff

All except one of the twelve credit unions studied in detail had some kind of premises from which to conduct their business. Three of the larger unions, in Northern Ireland, had bought their own offices. Three unions used the church hall, and two a local community centre. One credit union based on a housing estate had campaigned for use of the lock-ups below the blocks of flats and had managed to convert them into adequate business premises. One of the work-based groups had its own office and part-time manager heavily subsidised by the employer. The other operated from the desks of its elected officers and three regular collection points in different office buildings. In the credit union with no premises, all business was conducted from the homes of committee members or collectors.

The availability of premises could have an important influence on the structure of a credit union. There was a limit on the scale of operation that could be maintained from premises hired for the evening. On the other hand, a very large membership would be required to sustain a permanent office.

> Not having your own premises plays a big part in keeping your membership down. You don't have the facilities for storage to begin with, for keeping all your stationery and account books. The amount of work we're doing now is enough to keep us going at the

rate we're going now. If you did have premises of your own you
would have to have a larger membership to pay for the premises.

Unions with their own premises had acquired the full range of
office furnishings: desks, typewriters, telephones, photocopiers,
computing facilities, storage and filing systems; the workplace credit
unions had access to most of these things at work. Some other credit
unions had bought one or more items of equipment, or used facilities
available at their meeting place. But many relied on resources
available to individual committee members – their home telephone or
the photocopier available at their place of work. For two credit unions
storage was a particular problem. The membership and accounting
records had to be carried to and from collections in suitcases.

Business hours fell into one of two types of arrangement. The
work-based groups and those with permanent premises and/or paid
staff could offer a service more like a bank. Members could pay in
their savings, or go to negotiate a loan, during regular weekday
opening hours, and often with the added advantage of a Saturday
morning session. The smaller community based unions, though, were
open for business only at specific times – usually Friday evenings. All
members were expected to pay in their savings at this time, and the
social aspect of the session was felt to stimulate group loyalty. One
union supplemented the Friday session with a collection on Sunday
morning and Monday evening as well.

Although responsibility for the management of credit unions
invariably rests with a board or committee of members, both the
legislation and the model rules of the umbrella organisations allow
staff to be employed.

The decision whether to hire staff will usually be dictated by the
size of the union. A group with a few hundred members would neither
need paid assistance nor be able to afford it; one with thousands of
members would have sufficient resources to cover the costs, and could
not be administered without staff. It is, however, an over-
simplification to think in terms of a single point of decision – while
there will be a level of assets below which it would be unthinkable to
employ someone, and another level above which it would be
unavoidable, there will be a range within which the decision will
depend on the policy and circumstances of the management group.

ILCU reports that there are 800 paid staff working for credit unions
in Ireland, north and south of the border. Our own figures are based

on expenditure on salaries rather than on a direct head-count, but it can be seen that employment of staff was normal in Northern Ireland, and rare in Great Britain. The difference is partly explained by the relative numbers of large and small unions on each side side of the water, but credit unions of a given size were still more likely to hire workers in Northern Ireland than in Great Britain.

**Table 2.1    Proportion of unions reporting any expenditure on salaries, by number of members**

*Percentages*

| Number of members | Total | Up to 149 | 150 to 499 | 500 to 999 | 1000 to 1999 | 2000 or more |
|---|---|---|---|---|---|---|
| Great Britain | 15 | 3 | 19 | 45 | 33 | na |
| Northern Ireland | 80 | na | 38 | 86 | 95 | 100 |

One set of questions about the hiring of staff was purely practical. The total amount of work that could be achieved by volunteers on their own was limited. Paid assistance therefore enabled a union run on a larger scale than would otherwise have been possible. The additional labour could also be used to promote the union within the community defined by the common bond, and this might increase the membership. The disadvantage of paying staff, of course, was the cost; money spent on salaries would raise operating expenses and therefore reduce the surplus available for dividends and reserves. If, on the other hand, the staff's additional work enabled the union to gain or retain a larger membership than volunteers could service, the salaries would be self-financing: more members meant more income-generating assets.

But many of the leaders who had considered the possibility of taking on paid assistance were concerned more with the style and image of the credit union than with immediately practical matters. One question, which will be discussed in more detail in the next section, was about the size of the group; those who preferred a small, tightly-knit union preferred not to hire staff because that would have increased the pressure for growth. But paid workers might also have an effect of their own on the relationship between the members, committee members and the institution. The argument is typical of wider debates about the relative merits of voluntarism and professionalism.

Some people felt that credit unions with staff were efficient, businesslike, serving the community as a whole, competing, perhaps, with bigger institutions like banks and building societies. These attributes were admired by many of the people we spoke to. Paid staff freed volunteers from the routine operations of the credit union, allowing them to concentrate on higher order tasks such as planning and policy-making. The reduction in the amount of time required of elected members might also increase the number of talented people who would be prepared to come forward.

But others disagreed: they felt that staff could undermine the elected leaders' involvement in running the union, to the extent that they would spend more time worrying about the staff than about policy. A professional management might set its own interests above the welfare of individual members. It was also felt that the instinctive loyalty of grass-roots members would be diminished if they dealt with employees rather than with volunteers drawn from among their own ranks. If this affected members' savings and repayment habits, the cost might be high.

> We would feel as if we would lose the whole environment of our own credit union, where it's all voluntary. We enjoy the idea of it all being voluntary and us giving up our time to run the credit union. The main thing in credit unions is the personal touch. You have voluntary staff who are there because they want to be there and therefore they are going to give more to the community. I think we would lose out because the volunteers would back out if someone was getting paid to do it.

From the committee members' personal point of view, the trade-off was between a heavy burden of unpaid work on the one hand, and a loss of direct involvement in the affairs of the union on the other. A particular problem for many of the groups lay in their own inexperience of recruiting and supervising subordinates. There was a risk of hiring an unsuitable person, or of officers' delegating too much or too little of their work. Indeed, even among committee members who had debated the possibility of hiring staff, few appeared to have thought clearly about the role that they would assign to an employee – whether clerical assistance under the direct supervision of officers who would retain day to day control, or managerial responsibility reporting to the committee at intervals.

Much of the discussion of the possibilities and potential difficulties of hiring staff came from the leaders of unions which were not really in a position to do so. Among the twelve unions studied in detail, the largest, with many thousands of members, employed a manager who led a substantial team of full and part time staff. As would be expected, this manager was given a fairly free hand to run things as he saw fit and to refer problems back to the Board.

> A management committee has to stand back and let the manager do the managing. It would be very unfair of us to come and dictate to the manager all the time exactly what should be happening with his staff. The manager is running the place according to the way the Board wants it run.

Although, as some elected officers said:

> It's not as exciting now as it was in the early stages. It's very mundane.

Another credit union, based in the workplace, had taken on a part-time administrator paid for by the employer. The administrator arrived at a time when the credit union was close to collapse, and the volunteers were unable to cope with the demands being placed upon them. For the elected officers, the administrator had now become essential:

> You'd need a small committee of five or six people to even half way get to grips with the work that Sue does. It would be practically impossible. It would be every lunch hour. Without Sue the credit union would have been defunct a long time ago. If you haven't got the skills I think it's perfectly in order to buy those skills in. At the moment we can't afford Sue's skills. We've offered to make a contribution, and if we increase our membership we can buy them.

But the administrator felt that her presence had led to a lack of commitment from volunteers and that they were now much less willing to put in the time necessary to help manage the credit union.

Two other members of the sample had previous experience of subsidised staff. One had benefitted from a GLC programme which provided managers for five credit unions to help build up membership and resources to the point at which the unions could pay the manager's salary themselves. The 95% initial subsidy was phased out completely over three years. The scheme is said to have been successful in two cases, both of which had common bonds based on a previously existing association; but it was not a success among the other three, community-based, credit unions. This might mean that the outsider had prevented the development of group loyalty through participation which is thought to be so crucial to the success of a small union. The officers of the one in our sample said that there had been some practical advantages:

> The credit union premises could be opened during the day ... We were doing a publicity drive and he dropped a lot of leaflets in doors ... He used to help with the monthly statements. His main job was that everything should be prepared. When we came at nights all we would have to do is to sign up and agree and see that everything is done.

But it did not work out, perhaps because the committee were put under pressure to take decisions in time for a deadline:

> We had no experience, we had never before done that, hired somebody. We didn't really know what the job involved. We didn't have a clear idea of what we wanted. The candidates we managed to get, it was difficult to really size them up and feel if they were going to help or in which way they would help.

The person they chose had no previous experience of credit unions and no commitment to them. The officers, inexperienced though they were, had to train him. In the end:

> The subsidy ... was another trap, because we got used to him on a subsidised basis. The moment we had to start paying some of his salary, we found it was really difficult and we had to stop. It was a disservice as it turned out.

Another credit union had employed an MSC worker for one year. Again, it did not work out:

> I think she was grossly underused for her skills because the Treasurer kept her on a very tight rein. The Treasurer we had at that time was not willing to let her into it and she became very disillusioned.

These examples suggest that small credit unions should approach the possibility of hired help with caution, even if the initial costs would be borne by someone else. Well-trained and well-managed employees might provide continuity and technical skills, improving the quality of service and stimulating growth. In some situations it may be essential – the credit union currently being set up for employees of Birmingham Council has 1,200 members waiting to join, and a full-time manager will be necessary from day one. But a paid manager does not appear to be an automatic solution, and a badly planned move could prove disastrous.

## The question of growth

It has already been reported that the two organisations which represent credit unions in Great Britain differ in their views about the ideal size of a credit union and the strategy for expansion. The Association of British Credit Unions emphasises financial objectives, and aims for fewer, larger and more business-like unions. The National Federation emphasises objectives such as self-help and community development, and aims for a large number of unions, each of them confined to a few hundred members.

A parallel but not identical set of questions faced the leaders of individual credit unions once they had established themselves: should they aim to grow, or stay small? There were advantages and problems associated with each option.

### *Staying small*

People had different ideas about the dividing line between large and small unions. But many felt that they should not exceed 800 members – about the number at which it became necessary to consider employing staff. Some preferred to remain smaller than that, putting the optimum size around the 200 mark. The advantages of smallness lay in the personal contact among members and officers, which was said to strengthen group loyalty. There were practical advantages if this loyalty stimulated regular savings patterns and a low level of bad debt. But the proponents of smallness appeared to value the group ethic for its own sake, at least as much as for any effect on the finances of the union. The fact that members were helping themselves and each other by their own will and out of their own resources was 'the whole point' of having a credit union; it would be lost if members no longer felt actively involved in its management.

Other leaders took the opposite view. But those who preferred to remain small faced some problems. First, the policy was at odds with the desire of all credit union advocates to spread the benefits of membership to as many people as possible. It was hard to turn people away, or even to go slow on promoting the union. The alternative was to start another union, but this was never easy, especially if the new union was intended to recruit within the same common bond. So far as is known, unions have never tried the growth-of-cell strategy of growing to a certain size and then splitting into two.

Staying at a preferred size might also lead to a series of problems associated with stagnation. There were practical difficulties involved in trying retain a fixed number of members: the block on recruitment would lead to an 'aging' and inward-looking membership, into which it could be difficult to draft new people to replace those who left. The union affairs might be left more and more to a small group of people, again with difficulties if some of the leading members tried to 'retire'. And it might be difficult to maintain a healthy financial structure without resort to artificial means – requesting members to save or to borrow more or less, not for their own benefit but simply in support of the union. These are not inevitable consequences of a decision to remain small, but they are risks which must become more serious as time goes by.

A small union would have a small financial base and low reserves. On the other hand, the strong group loyalty and the lack of fixed operating costs might enable it to respond flexibly to a crisis, as long as it did not offer any large loans. It is not clear, therefore, whether a stable small group would face higher or lower financial risks than a large one.

### Trying to grow
Whatever the arguments for or against large credit unions, a second set of problems was associated with the attempt to make the transition from small to large. First, there was a general difficulty in recruiting more people to join a group which was not widely known or understood. While the first few hundred members might be contacted by word of mouth along existing grapevines, later stages of expansion might require different methods. But, as some officers pointed out, publicity on a wider scale could lead to creating the impression that credit unions could provide instant access to cheap credit for the public at large without the necessary preliminaries of membership and regular savings. And the group identity that had been so helpful in the initial stages might limit the scope for recruitment later on.

> Even when you push them personally, as soon as you say a loan, they say 'I won't get into debt'. You really need a friend, people that you know, and explain to them. Even then it's hard. We've had it announced from the pulpit. We've had it in the bulletin. We had an article for the newspaper, and we had two requests to buy cars overnight, which we turned down. It's very difficult to get

through what it's really about. They don't really believe what you're saying in the leaflets and so on. It doesn't really get across.

A second hindrance to growth was the increasing amount of work which had to be done by the leadership group, not only to recruit new members, but also to service their savings and loans. Over-rapid expansion had caused one union serious problems:

> The trouble was we were rushed off our feet because we found there was an almost instant demand for the services we were providing and we hadn't got ourselves geared up to deal with it adequately. The people trying to run it lacked skills and the credit union came close to collapse ... Our membership was falling because we weren't able to offer the service that the members wanted. It developed a poor reputation so it made it very difficult to gain new members. It's not that anything dishonest ever took place, it was just an inability of some people involved to cope with the demands.

But several others had developed a policy for controlled expansion:

> We have never gone out and had a publicity campaign to get people in because we could get them in. The question you then have to ask is, if you get them in, can you service them? The chances are if you get a hundred members, there's a hundred people who have a need and you're getting that need right away. So we feel we have to let the growth come naturally, so we can control it and ... service it.

As the membership and the workload grew, the limitations of voluntary workers operating in hired premises became more serious.

> Not having your own premises plays a big part in keeping your membership down ... You don't have the facilities for storage to begin with ... If you did have premises of your own you would have to have a larger membership to pay for the premises.

> The only advantage of growing for me is that you're giving the benefit of the service to more people. Obviously the more people you have, the more time it takes to administer and it puts greater strains on the people who are doing it, who are basically doing it voluntarily anyway. There is a point you must reach where you get to that size where you're actually talking about having professional people doing it on a full-time basis.

Although one of the unions in the sample was successfully servicing over 1,000 members on an entirely voluntary basis, it will be seen that there is a natural hump in the growing process, at the point where the volunteers and the premises cannot cope with any further increase. At this point the union probably cannot support permanent premises and/or full-time staff, but these services would repay their cost if they enabled the union to grow further.

While few British credit unions have managed to pass this hump, most of those in Northern Ireland have done so, to stabilise with thousands of members and substantial assets. None of them has reached anything like the scale of some of the huge American credit unions, or of the British building societies, though that may simply reflect the small population of the Province. Both of those examples lead to the possibility that a further stage in credit union development might be a series of mergers into larger, more efficiently administered, but inevitably more impersonal institutions.

The leaders of those unions which had expanded were conscious of the reduction in personal contact between members that this had involved. But, though they regretted that there was no longer so much fun to be had, they did not think that it undermined the service that was being provided to their members. Nevertheless, people were worried about the effects of getting larger. No-one wanted to become just another commercial organisation:

> The credit unions in Australia and Canada work a cheque system just like any other financial institution. You can go to them and they have an auto-teller out in the street. Now that's how they envisage us being eventually. That's not a vision I have of it. It's a vision that some directors do have of it, but then I don't think we're any better than the financial institutions that are causing mayhem with the plastic card. I don't want a credit union with a plastic card because I think that's not any different from having a TSB plastic card. They think this is the way to go, but for me it's not the way to go.

# 3. Joining a Credit Union

The previous chapter examined some of the issues facing the people trying to set up and manage credit unions. The focus now turns to the members. What sort of people were they; how had they come to join the union; what did they hope to get out of it? There is a big change of gear in the presentation of the findings at this point. Earlier discussion has relied largely on evidence provided by individuals with experience of promoting or managing credit unions. This chapter, and the following two, are based on interviews with 231 ordinary members, using a formal questionnaire. The results of this survey appear in the form of tables showing how many people gave one reply or the other, rather than quotations of the views of individuals. The survey method has been summarised in the Introduction; more technical details appear in the Appendix.

The survey covered about 33 members of each of seven credit unions. Some of the findings apply equally to all seven; but in other respects, the groups turned out to be very different from each other. This diversity means that the experience of any one union may not be typical, and it is difficult to reach general conclusions about 'credit unions' as a breed. Constant comparison is needed between the different experiences. This is quite hard work for both the analyst and the reader, and it may help to try to fix the seven unions in the mind before proceeding to detailed analysis. The seven have not been identified, in order to protect the anonymity of our informants. Instead, they have been given names which indicate roughly whereabouts they were. All the charts in the following three chapters present the seven unions in the same order. The list starts with the 'richest' unions, as measured by the incomes of their members, and ends with the 'poorest'.

**Suburb:** *A long-established credit union in a prosperous London suburb, based on a Catholic parish, but not confined to members of the Church.*

**Borough:** *A credit union organised among the employees of an urban local authority. This is the only employment-based union in the survey.*

**Yorkshire:** *Another church-based union in a residential area of a medium-sized town.*

**Belfast:** *A union established across the sectarian divide in Northern Ireland.*

**N. Ireland:** *A large, professionally administered credit union, also in Northern Ireland. Like most unions there, linked to the Catholic Church.*

**Northern:** *A small and recently established credit union in an inner city housing estate.*

**Scotland:** *Another union based on a poor estate, this one in Scotland.*

Readers may find it helpful to put a bookmark in this page of the report, so that they can use the outline description of the credit unions as a point of reference through the remainder of the analysis.

## Members
### *Economic circumstances*
In one sense, all sorts of people join credit unions. The survey identified bank managers, solicitors and company directors; cleaners and dustmen; retired, sick and unemployed people. Looking at all seven unions, the jobs of the members* were as follows:

| | |
|---|---|
| Professional or managerial | 17 per cent |
| Clerical | 16 per cent |
| Skilled manual | 19 per cent |
| Semi- or unskilled | 17 per cent |
| Retired | 10 per cent |
| Others not in work | 21 per cent |

---

\* For married couples, we have analysed the occupation of the partner with the higher earnings; usually but not always the husband.

But although the sample as a whole was a broad cross-section of society, each union recruited its members from a rather narrower spectrum (Chart 3.1). At one extreme, two-thirds of the members of the Suburb credit union were in professional or managerial jobs. None of the others had more than a seventh of their members in these senior occupations. At the other end of the scale, the N. Ireland union, and the two groups established on inner city housing estates (Northern and Scotland) included large proportions of unemployed or otherwise unoccupied people. In the middle of the range, three unions drew the majority of their members from among clerical and manual workers.

**Chart 3.1   Work of chief economic supporter: members of different credit unions**

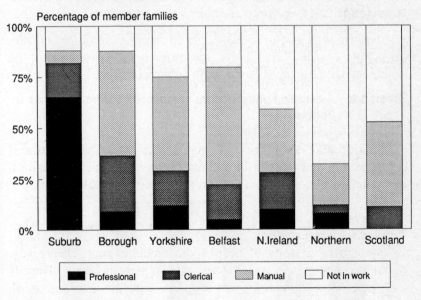

A family's income depends partly on the occupation of the chief economic supporter, but also on possible earnings of his or her spouse, and on taxes paid and social security benefits received. Throughout this report, we have compared the net income of each family in the sample with the supplementary benefit ordinary scale rates in force at the time of the survey, plus housing costs. (The benefit system changed in April 1988; the supplementary benefit ordinary rates are roughly equivalent to the income support basic rate for people aged 25 to 59.)

This comparison takes account of variations in family size, and effectively shows how far each family was above or below the minimum income specified by the government. For example, a married couple with a child in primary school, paying £30 per week in rent and rates, would have been entitled to a basic £59.75 per week in benefits at the time of the survey; if one of the families in our sample fitted this description but had a net income of £139.75 per week, the family's 'available income' would be calculated to be £50.

The average 'available income' of union members' families was £68 per week:

- the richest quarter of the sample had an available income above £110 per week.
- the poorest quarter had an available income of less than £10 per week.

Even though income (measured in this way) is not simply a matter of people's wages and salaries, the differences between the credit unions stand out again (Chart 3.2). In Suburb, only one member of the

**Chart 3.2   Available family income: members of different credit unions.**

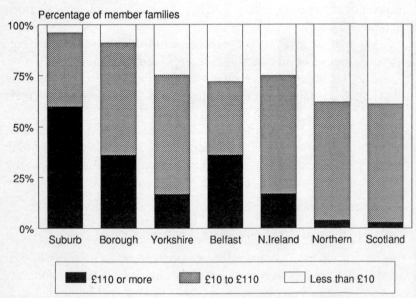

Note:   'Available income' is calculated as the difference between the family's net income and the supplementary benefit scale rate.

sample was anywhere near the poverty line; the majority had an income at least £110 clear of their basic needs. None of the other credit unions came near this level of prosperity. At the other end of the spectrum, over a third of the members of the Northern and Scotland unions had barely enough to live on, and hardly any were in the comfortable income bracket enjoyed by many of those in the Suburb union.

So, even though people from all walks of life are prepared to join a credit union, there was rather a strong tendency for people in similar circumstances to join each other. This concentration may reflect the common bond which is a central element of the credit union concept. It has some important implications both for the finances and the management of the unions, however. A large proportion of the people with plenty of money were recycling it within a single union, for other people with plenty of money to borrow. Meanwhile the majority of the unemployed and other poor people in the sample were members of two unions where they had to rely on each others' meagre resources to build up a savings and loans fund. It may also be assumed that the 'richest' union had a large reserve of people with managerial and financial experience to help run the union, while most of the rest, especially the two poorest, would have had to learn these tasks from scratch.

Much of the analysis in the remainder of this report will focus on the experiences of members at different levels of income.

Another indicator of people's economic circumstances is their housing. Nationally, more than 60 per cent of all households own their own home. Among credit unions, just under half (47 per cent) of the householders in the sample were owner-occupiers; most of the rest were council tenants. But the full range was between 89 per cent home ownership in Suburb, to none at all in the housing estate on which the Scotland union was based. Chart 3.3 shows that not many of the council employees belonging to the Borough credit union were owner-occupiers; otherwise, the pattern between unions closely followed the analysis of employment and income.

**Chart 3.3    Housing tenure: members of different credit unions.**

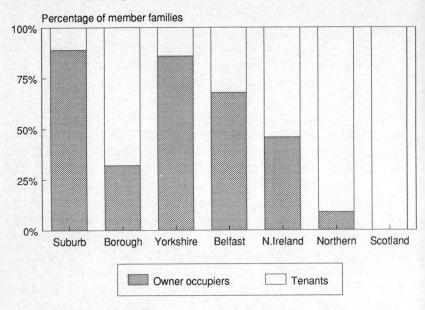

Note:    Chart confined to householdsers.

## *Demographic characteristics*

Four of the credit unions had been set up by, or with the support of, the Catholic Church. Two of these, including the large union in N. Ireland, were (almost) exclusively confined to Catholics; the other two defined their common bond in such a way as to include other people, and about a quarter of their members were non-Catholics (Chart 3.4). The two British unions which had no direct connection with the Catholic Church nevertheless found that a significant minority of their members were Catholics. But in Northern Ireland, the Belfast credit union which had been set up deliberately to embrace both Catholics and Protestants turned out to consist mostly of Protestants. This was surprising, since its leaders had told the researcher that their membership split about half and half. Perhaps the Catholics within this union's catchment area were already members of other credit unions.

**Chart 3.4    Religious denomination: members of different credit unions.**

Only 14 per cent of credit union members were over the age of 60, compared with 21 per cent of the adult population, and it appears that elderly and retired people are relatively unlikely to join. Otherwise, the membership was evenly spread across age-groups.

Many of the credit unions had recruited a large proportion of women among their members. Taking the members of all seven unions together:

- 16 per cent were non-married men;
- 17 per cent were married men whose wife had not joined;
- 18 per cent were married couples, both of whom had joined;
- 21 per cent were married women, whose husband had not joined;
- 27 per cent were non-married women (including many lone mothers).

Not surprisingly, there were no members of the workplace-based union (Borough) who reported that their spouse was also a member. This was the only union where men predominated (Chart 3.5). Among the community based groups, the two oldest established (Suburb and N. Ireland) had a large number of married couples, both of whom had joined the union; here (and also in Belfast) there was a fairly even balance between men and women in the membership as a whole. But at the remaining three unions, more than half of the members were women who were either not married, or whose husband had not joined. The predominance of women was particularly marked in the two poorest unions (Northern and Scotland), reflecting, perhaps, the heavy responsibilities for budget management carried by women in poor families.*

**Chart 3.5   Sex and marital status: members of different credit unions.**

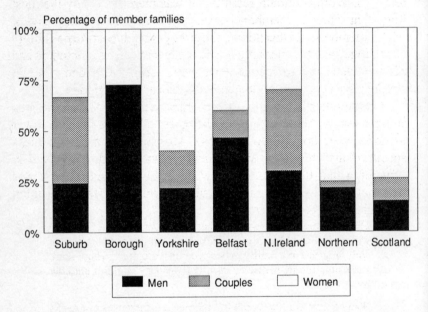

Note:   'Men' includes single men, and also husbands whose wives have not joined; 'women' similarly; 'couples' means husbands and wives who have both joined.

## Joining the credit union
Among the seven unions covered by the survey, the N. Ireland and Suburb unions had been set up a long time ago: on average, their members had been with the union more than ten years. The remainder

---

*   Among married couples, only 14 per cent of the wives of professional and managerial workers had joined the credit union on their own, without their husband. This rose to 30 per cent of the wives of clerical workers; 44 per cent of the wives of manual workers and 51 per cent of the wives of men without employment.

were more recently established, and the average member had joined between two and four years before being interviewed.

Some members had found out about the credit union by receiving a personal visit, seeing an advertisement or poster or reading a leaflet. Most of the members recruited by these slightly formal methods came from two credit unions (Borough and Northern), one of which was the workplace union which would have had convenient methods of internal communication. But the overwhelming majority of members – four out of five – had heard about their union from friends or relatives. Word of mouth recruitment was therefore easily the most important source of members – even for the very largest union, all of whose members said that this was how they came across the possibility of joining. That does not necessarily mean that existing members had actively gone out to recruit newcomers; successful unions might simply have become well-known within local communities.

On the other hand, a lot of members were not keen on the idea straight away. About a third of them, especially those with lower incomes, were doubtful to start with. Most of them did not express specific fears; they were simply nervous about getting involved in something that they did not know much about. And often it was personal contact – with another member or with an officer of the union – which helped to set their mind at ease.

> I think people just don't believe that it's as simple as it is. I suppose we're conditioned to being bombarded with things being simple and they are not really when you investigate. They think something run by perhaps a group of amateurs couldn't possibly be successful.

> Many a time we said 'wouldn't it be nice if there was one here'. But then it took me a while to come in when it did start because I didn't really know who was involved in it. Then I went into it in more detail and was visited by a committee member who explained it.

When they were asked why they had joined, most members referred to one or other of the two obvious attributes of a credit union. Nearly half said that they were attracted by the opportunity to make regular savings:

> I wanted to save small amounts. I would not go to a bank with £2.

> It was convenient. It's just down the stairs from here. A handy way to save.

And more than a third mentioned the chance of borrowing. Many of these specifically mentioned the low rate of interest paid on credit union loans:

> The interest is low. It doesn't cripple you repaying it. You don't stay awake all night thinking of all the interest clocking up, which I do if I have an overdraft.

> Everybody is living on credit and this is the cheapest credit of everybody in fact. And not only that, I think people once they've got the idea, are quite happy to save, to help to use their money to be used to help other people.

Various other specific advantages of the credit union were each mentioned by smaller numbers of members – the convenience of local collections, the ease and speed with which loans could be arranged and the friendly and sympathetic way people were treated:

> The insurance is a big thing. I won't benefit because I'll be buried but my family will maybe benefit whenever I pass away.

> I think it's a feeling that you know it's there. Even if you're not in the middle of a crisis, you know that if anything did happen you've got something to fall back.

Finally, one in ten had been drawn in by the idealism of the credit union movement:

> (I joined) in order to help the community and local people in the parish and to get rid of loan sharks.

> You're helping yourself to help other people. With being a member the money is there for you to borrow as well as for everybody else to borrow.

People's motives varied quite strongly, both between unions, and according to their economic circumstances. They were asked to say whether they were more interested in saving or in borrowing when they joined. Table 3.6* compares the answers of people at different levels of income. Relatively poor people were much more likely to be interested in saving then in borrowing; relatively rich people were more attracted by the credit facility than the savings scheme. This is a large difference, and suggests important conclusions about people's approach to the movement.

---

\* Note that Charts and Tables have a single sequence of numbers, so that Table 3.6 follows Chart 3.5.

**Table 3.6  Main motive for joining, by family income**

*Percentage of members*

| Available family income | Total | Less than £10 pw | £10 to £49 | £50 to £109 | £110 or more |
|---|---|---|---|---|---|
| To save | 53 | 65 | 55 | 56 | 36 |
| To borrow | 41 | 30 | 38 | 33 | 59 |
| Both or neither | 6 | 5 | 7 | 11 | 4 |
| (Sample size) | (231) | (53) | (58) | (58) | (62) |

Chart 3.7 compares the motives of members of the different unions. These seemed to be linked to the economic circumstances of the members, but that was not the whole story, and each union appeared to have an ethos of its own. It is hard to believe that all these groups belong to the same movement, their members' motivations were so different. At one union, eight out of ten members were principally attracted by the opportunity to borrow money; altogether, three unions were found to be based predominantly on this motive. But the members of the other four unions were mainly interested in saving.

## Training members

A 'good' member of a credit union was...

> ... someone who saves regularly, borrows wisely and repays on time and therefore has a good understanding of how the credit union works and the principles behind it.

And to encourage a 'good' membership officers aimed to explain to joiners at an early stage the purpose and function of a credit union. This could involve a one-to-one chat with an officer or another member or attendance at education sessions which were held at regular intervals. Attending such a session could be made a condition of granting the first loan.

> On the night we get them, we sit down and we take as much time as is needed to try and explain to them properly. We feel that if you don't get them on the first night and let them know what a credit union is, you've lost them.

> Somebody is recommended and we say okay, buy the handbook and read it first and then we'll come and talk to you. So at least

**Chart 3.7   Main motive for joining, by family income**

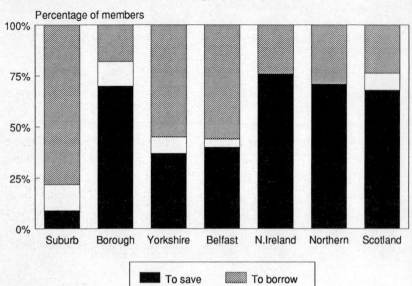

having read the handbook they've got the outline of the philosophy
and the method, how it works.

But officers found that it was not until members began to make full
use of the services that they really began to understand how the union
worked.  In particular joiners often had problems in understanding
why they should take out a loan rather than use their savings.

Mary's mother was in it.  She didn't like the borrowing aspect of
it. She hated it.  She couldn't understand it at all.  She wanted to
go to Ireland but she just didn't want a loan, she wanted her savings.

Nine out of ten people I speak to, they don't really understand what
the credit union is about until they have joined and started to
borrow and started to pay back and all of a sudden the penny drops.
They become thrifty because it's so important for them to save.  If
they don't save, it means that they think we're moneylenders.  But
it's usually once they start to borrow and pay back and start saving
they say 'I know now what you were getting at at the beginning'.
They usually stay quite loyal.

**Involvement in union activities**

The survey of credit union members included interviews with some committee members and officers who happened to be selected in the random sample, so they can be compared with the 'ordinary' members. 24 members of the sample were found to be 'leaders' – that is, they were current committee members or officers, or they had been in the past, or they were one of the people who had helped to set the union up in the first place. The leadership group therefore represented about 10 per cent of all members. The survey confirmed that there was a fair degree of continuity in the leadership group. More than half of those who had ever been leaders held office at the time they were interviewed. One third of the leadership group appeared to have held office ever since they had joined the union; another third had been leaders for at least half of their period of membership. But there was no sign that their work was a burden to them; some said they would be prepared to put in more time on union affairs, none said they wanted to cut down on their involvement.

Some leaders were keen to build up a cadre of potential committee members by involving rank and file members in various tasks such as collecting money, making tea, introducing new members and so on. Leaving aside the leadership group, about 5 per cent of members said that they were 'helpers' of one sort or another. Another 8 per cent said that they would be interested in helping in some way, and may be considered potential recruits. The majority of those expressing this interest, however, had never attended any of the meetings arranged for the union's members, and it may be doubted how eager they would be in practice.

Most unions organise regular collection sessions, at which members pay in their weekly or monthly savings instalments or loan repayments. Attending these (probably only for a few minutes) would be a normal part of the routine of membership. The survey asked questions about attendance at other types of meeting, to get an idea of the extent of ordinary people's involvement. Table 3.8 suggests a big cleavage between the leadership group and the rank and file. The leaders reported regular attendance at the AGM; most had been to social gatherings; and many of them had attended education sessions and other types of meeting. But 'ordinary' members were much less likely to have been to sessions of this kind. At a rough estimate, about half of the people at one of these meetings would turn out to be drawn

**Table 3.8    Attendance at meetings: leaders compared with rank and file**

*Percentage of members*

|  | Total | Leaders | Rank and file |
|---|---|---|---|
| **Annual general meeting** | | | |
| Regularly | 12 | 72 | 5 |
| Sometimes | 9 | 15 | 8 |
| Rarely/just once | 11 | - | 12 |
| Never | 69 | 13 | 75 |
| **Education sessions** | | | |
| Ever attended | 17 | 40 | 15 |
| **Social gatherings** | | | |
| Ever attended | 20 | 78 | 14 |
| **Other meetings for members** | | | |
| Ever attended | 9 | 53 | 4 |
| (Sample size) | (231) | (24) | (207) |

from the leadership group. Although most of the meetings are intended to draw the rank and file into closer involvement with the union, nearly two-thirds of them (63 per cent) had never been to any of them.

This apparent lack of involvement of ordinary members in the affairs of their credit union contrasted strongly with the ideals of mutual aid and empowerment expressed by the leaders of the movement. Some of the people quoted in the last chapter felt that ordinary members would feel separated from the management if credit unions were allowed to get too large. But the comparison in Chart 3.9 does not particularly suggest that size was the most important factor. N. Ireland was easily the largest group covered by the survey, and about half of its members had attended meetings; the smallest in the survey was Northern, and hardly any of its members had attended meetings.

**Chart 3.9    Attendance at meetings: members of different credit unions**

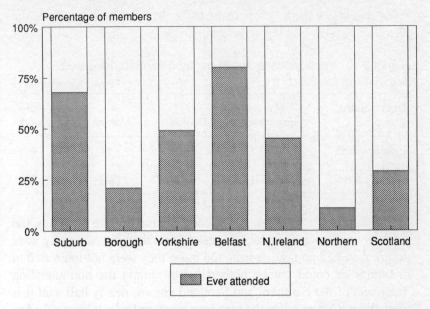

Given the many differences between unions, it is difficult to identify the reasons for the variation in member-involvement. It seems likely, however, that the low participation rate in Borough was associated with its base in the workplace. The members saw it as a service provided by their employer, and would have considered attendance at meetings or other involvement in union affairs almost as a form of overtime. (We experienced great difficulty in obtaining interviews from members of this credit union, for the same reason.) It might be argued that if employment provides a strong enough common bond, the credit union could remain viable without active participation by its members.

But the other two unions with low participation rates (Northern and Scotland) were based on inner city housing estates, and might have been expected to have depended very heavily on member involvement to maintain the bond. These were the two groups dominated by low-paid and unemployed families, whose experience in other spheres of life may have made it difficult to believe that their opinions would be taken into consideration. Table 3.10 suggests that participation in union activities was quite strongly linked to income and class: the better-off, middle class members more likely to attend meetings than poor people. The table may not be surprising, but it might be a disappointment to the proponents of credit unions as agents in the development of working class communities.

**Table 3.10  Attendance at meetings, by occupational group**

*Percentage of members*

| Occupational group | Manager Professional | Clerical | Manual | Not in work |
|---|---|---|---|---|
| Ever attended | 73 | 42 | 44 | 27 |
| (Sample size) | (38) | (37) | (84) | (72) |

When people were asked why they had not been to meetings, the majority gave reasons which suggested that they did not really want to go: they had no time or were too busy; they were not interested in meetings or could not be bothered. But among the non-attending members of the Northern and Scotland unions, nearly half said that they did not know when the meetings were, or had not been asked to any. In contrast, there were two unions (Belfast and N. Ireland) among whose members no-one pleaded ignorance in this way. The management of individual credit unions may therefore have a big effect on the participation rate of members, depending on the effectiveness of communications.

These measurements of participation are based on attendance at special meetings. Some unions, perhaps, placed much more emphasis in participation during the weekly collection services. Certainly, there was a real buzz of community spirit in evidence at the meeting of the Scotland union attended by the researcher – far greater than might have been expected from its low rating in Chart 3.9.

There were few signs that non-participation led to dissatisfaction or alienation. Hardly any (3 per cent) of the people interviewed said that they were at all dissatisfied with the way their credit union was run. The majority were 'very' satisfied, and commented on the efficiency of the organisation, the convenience of the arrangements, the availability of low interest credit, and the friendly, welcoming atmosphere.

I think the system for collecting is first class and also all the paperwork. It's really above board and well administered.

The people in the office are very friendly and make you feel welcome, unlike other places where you get interrogated.

The interest is good and the arrangements for loans are very good.

Although almost everyone was satisfied with the way their union was run, less than half of those who had never attended a meeting were prepared to say they were 'very' satisfied, compared with nearly three-quarters of those who were more actively involved. There was also a sign of a connection between participation and enthusiasm when the unions were compared with each other. Chart 3.11 seems to show that those unions which attracted a lot of members to meetings received the most favourable assessments. But the two inner-city unions with a low participation rate got a better rating than would have been expected in comparison with the other five.

**Chart 3.11  Satisfaction with the way union is run: members of different unions**

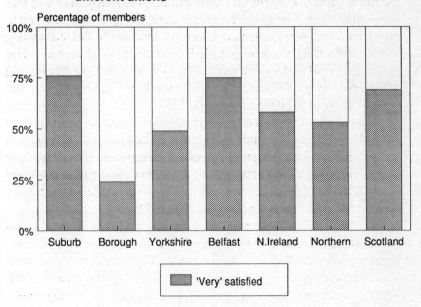

If there was little dissatisfaction with the way the union was run, nor was there much complaint about the balance of power between the leaders and the ordinary members.

- 64 per cent of members felt that it was the directors and committee members who had most influence over the credit union;
- 23 per cent thought it was ordinary members who had the most influence;
- 13 per cent thought power was shared equally between the leaders and the rank and file, or did not know.

Taking one group with another, the general conclusion was that directors and committee members had more say than ordinary members; but surprisingly it was those who rarely or never attended meetings who quite often asserted that the ordinary members held most power. And, although there were a few people who wanted the directors and committee members to allow the members more say in things, this view was held by the leaders more often than by the members themselves (Table 3.12).

Most members seemed to be happy to make use of their credit union's services, without getting involved in running it.

## Community spirit

Credit union partisans often suggest that this way of organising savings and loans provides extra benefits to members, besides the purely financial services which might be obtained from a bank or a

**Table 3.12 Opinions on the relative influence of committees and ordinary members, by level of involvement in union**

*Percentages of members*

| Level of involvement | Leaders | Regularly attended | Rarely attended | Never attended |
|---|---|---|---|---|
| *Who has most influence?* | | | | |
| Directors/committees | 85 | 71 | 63 | 59 |
| Ordinary members | 9 | 13 | 28 | 26 |
| *Should directors have less, members have more control?* | | | | |
| Yes | 37 | 12 | 11 | 8 |
| (Sample size) | (24) | (32) | (45) | (130) |

building society. The special ingredient is often referred to as 'community': a feeling among members that they are helping and supporting each other. Community is not easily measured, but the survey included some questions to indicate how people felt.

One indicator was people's reasons for joining the credit union in the first place. The majority said they joined because they thought that it would be helpful to them personally. But quite a few gave more outward-looking motives: they thought the union would be helpful to other people, or would get people together and create a community spirit. Similarly, when they were asked to choose:

- 53 per cent said they were interested in the credit union mainly because it was useful to themselves;
- 34 per cent said they were interested mainly in the help it could offer to other members; and
- 13 per cent said they were interested in both equally.

Rather less than half of the members thought that they had got to know more people as a result of joining the credit union:

- 19 per cent knew lots more people;
- 22 per cent some more people; but
- 59 per cent knew no more people.

Considering themselves personally:

- 30 per cent felt that the union had 'definitely' helped to give them a feeling of belonging;
- 26 per cent felt this 'slightly'; but
- 43 per cent did not feel it at all.

But thinking about the members generally, people were more optimistic:

- 50 per cent said that the union had 'definitely' given its members a feeling of belonging and of community spirit;
- 23 per cent felt this 'slightly';
- 14 per cent said it had 'not really' happened; while
- 8 per cent said it had 'definitely not' happened.

Taking these four questions together, there is clear evidence of a degree of community spirit within credit unions, though it may not be as powerful as some leaders of the movement would hope and claim. Rather than analyse each of the four questions in detail, it is useful to combine the answers into a single measure of members' views on this subject. The technique identifies one-quarter of members whose combined answers showed most signs of community spirit, and one-quarter who showed fewest signs. These are labelled 'high' and 'low' levels of community spirit, though it is important to remember that these are simply defined in comparison with other members of the sample; they should be interpreted as meaning 'relatively high' and 'relatively low'.

Table 3.13 shows that the level of 'community spirit' expressed by credit union members was closely connected with the extent of their involvement in union activities. 'Leaders' were more conscious of the mutual support provided by credit unions than rank and file members

**Table 3.13  Level of community spirit, by level of involvement**

*Percentage of members*

| Level of involvement | Leader | Attended meetings | Never attended |
|---|---|---|---|
| High community spirit | 45 | 39 | 18 |
| Medium | 55 | 44 | 56 |
| Low community spirit | nil | 18 | 26 |
| Average score | 6.6 | 5.3 | 3.9 |
| (Sample size) | (24) | (77) | (130) |

Note:   Level of community spirit is derived from the answers to four questions. The average score is out of a maximum of ten.

were; and there was a similar difference between ordinary members who did and did not attend meetings such as the AGM. Although these differences were not unexpected, they help to emphasise the difference between the idealism often expressed by the movement's spokesmen and the more prosaic utilitarian approach of those who had joined a union for the services it provides.

'Community spirit' also varied widely from one credit union to another (Chart 3.14). The employment-based union (Borough) scored very low, and this was consistent with other indications of a weak sense of attachment among members of this group. One union (Scotland) stood out to show a much higher sense of community spirit than any of the others. This was in spite of the low level of attendance at the meetings of this group.

**Chart 3.14  Level of community spirit: members of different unions**

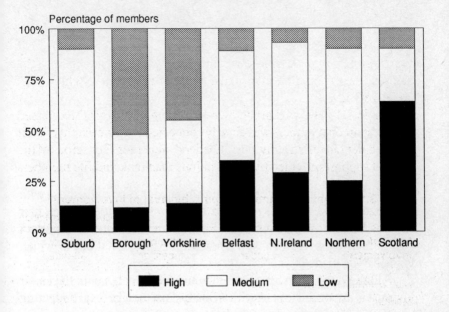

# 4. Savings

It has been seen that many credit union members, especially those with low incomes, were more attracted by the opportunities for regular savings than by the offer of loans. Savings are therefore an important aim in their own right, as well as providing the capital out of which loans can be made.

Although the main interest is in members' savings with the credit union, it is important to start with an analysis of their general budgeting position, and of their savings with other institutions.

## Budgeting

The interviews with credit union members included some general questions designed to indicate how members and their families were getting on with their budgeting from week to week and from month to month. People with high incomes and/or middle class jobs tended to budget by the month (if they had any regular system), while people relying on social security mostly worked by the week or fortnight. The proportion adopting weekly or two-weekly cycles ranged from nine out of ten in the two poorest unions (Northern and Scotland), to none at all in the richest (Suburb): a clear illustration of the variation in 'class' between one union and another. Similarly, the number of people with an ordinary current bank account, ranged from all the members of the richest, to only one in seven at the two poorest.

People taking part in the survey were asked three questions which would give an indication of how they were getting on financially.

- Do you ever manage to put money away at the end of each week/month?

  | | |
  |---|---|
  | Yes, most weeks | 37% |
  | More often than not | 9% |
  | Sometimes | 14% |
  | Hardly ever | 13% |
  | No, never | 28% |

- Do you ever run out of money before the end of the week/month?

  | | |
  |---|---|
  | Yes, most weeks | 13% |
  | More often than not | 17% |
  | Sometimes | 23% |
  | Hardly ever | 16% |
  | No, never | 31% |

- How are you managing on your money?

  | | |
  |---|---|
  | Managing quite well | 36% |
  | Just getting by | 55% |
  | Getting into difficulties | 9% |

In order to make comparisons between people in different circumstances, we have combined the answers to these three questions, so as to identify those families which found it relatively easy to budget (the 29 per cent of the sample who most often gave 'good' answers to these questions); and the those with difficulties (the 25 per cent who most often gave answers suggesting problems). As one would expect, people found it easier to budget the more income they had to budget with (Table 4.1). The same sequence of questions had been asked in another PSI survey which had covered a sample of supplementary benefit claimants: using the same definitions of 'easy to budget' and 'difficulties', the right hand column of the table shows that supplementary benefit claimants in general had similar budgeting experiences as the credit union members with incomes round about the supplementary benefit level (ie with an available income of less than £10) So there is little sign of credit union members having more or less of a problem than other people with similar resources.

It is to be expected that people's ability to budget would depend on two things: first, on the family's income in relation to its needs; and second, on a variety of individual circumstances including their particular style of management. Table 4.1 confirms that the family's income has a strong influence, though there were some people who

**Table 4.1   Budgeting experience, by available family income**

*Percentages of member-families*

| Available family income | Below £10 pw | £10 to £49 | £50 to £109 | £110 or more | (Sup Ben Clmts[1]) |
|---|---|---|---|---|---|
| Easy to budget | 14 | 17 | 42 | 41 | 15 |
| Neither easy nor difficult | 44 | 56 | 42 | 45 | 43 |
| Difficulties | 42 | 27 | 16 | 14 | 42 |
| (Sample size) | (55) | (59) | (59) | (57) | |

Note:   1.  See R. Berthoud, *The Reform of Supplementary Benefit*, Policy Studies Institute, 1984.

found it 'easy to budget' even on very low incomes, and others who experienced 'difficulties' even with high incomes. Any measure of the success with which people handle their money clearly has to take account of the amount of money they have in the first place. We looked carefully to see whether credit union members who experienced more or less budgeting difficulties than others with a similar level of income would save or borrow more or less than others. But no strong influences were to be found.

## Savings with other institutions

Credit unions exist within a general market of savings and credit opportunities provided by other institutions, which members are free to use.

- 34% of member-families had savings with a building society;
- 33% in a bank deposit account;
- 10% in a post office account; and
- 7% in other institutions, including unit trusts, stocks or shares.

Some families, of course, used more than one of these types of account. Looking at all four types of institution:

- 28% were making regular payments towards non-credit union savings;
- 33% had outside savings but were not making regular contributions;
- 15% had used one of these types of saving in the past, but no longer did so; and

• 23% said that they had never saved apart from with the credit union.

So three-fifths of members had outside savings at the time they were interviewed. The amounts ranged from less than £100 to well over £5,000. In fact all but one of the people with more than £5,000 outside savings were members of the same credit union (Suburb), the one whose members had also reported relatively high incomes. This one union averaged nearly £4,000 per head, and accounted for more than half of the non-credit union savings in the whole sample. In contrast the two 'poorest' unions had averages of only just over £100 each. The four unions which might be considered to be more typical averaged about £450 in outside savings per member.

**Table 4.2    Savings outside the credit union**

*Percentage of member-families*

|  | Richest union | Four middle unions | Two poorest unions |
|---|---|---|---|
| None | 15 | 40 | 58 |
| Up to £200 | 13 | 17 | 20 |
| £201 to £1000 | 15 | 27 | 23 |
| More than £1000 | 58 | 17 | nil |
| Average | £3,730 | £460 | £110 |
| (Sample size) | (33) | (132) | (66) |

Note:    The averages take into account those members who had no savings at all.

So availability of savings in building societies, banks and so on varied strongly from one credit union to another. Table 4.3 clearly shows how the extent of outside savings was determined by the economic position of the family, with averages ranging from more than £2,000 for senior non-manual workers, down to virtually nothing at all for the unemployed and lone parents. There is, in fact, little sign that the differences between the unions in their members' savings has anything to do with the unions themselves; the variation is entirely due to the differences in the circumstances of their members.

The existence of a pool of fairly substantial savings in building societies, banks and a few other places has important implications for

Table 4.3    Average non credit union savings, by economic position
of 'chief earner'

*Pounds*

| In full-time work | | Others | |
|---|---|---|---|
| Managerial and professional | £2,080 | Retired | £2,010 |
| Clerical | £900 | Sick/disabled | £240 |
| Skilled manual | £570 | PT work | £120 |
| Semi-skilled | £530 | Unemployed/ | |
| Unskilled | £90 | lone parents | £4 |

the evaluation of credit unions. It is just possible that some of these
savings have been assisted by the credit union itself: it might have
developed the saving habit in its members; the availability of loans
may have helped people to avoid withdrawing their outside savings to
meet short-term needs. But there is little direct evidence that members'
outside savings were more or less than they would have been if they
had never joined, and it is probably safest to assume that the pattern
is similar to what would have been observed in any case. If so, credit
unions had attracted many people who apparently had no need of a
new method of saving. At the same time, they failed to attract all of
the savings of those people.

Table 4.4 summarises the relative advantages and disadvantages
members ascribed to the credit union, compared with a building
society, as a place to save. There were two general advantages of a
credit union: convenience (such as the regular weekly paying-in
sessions organised by most unions); and the link between savings and
borrowing. Relatively few of the better-off members considered their
credit union a convenient method of saving, and this was only partially
off-set by a belief in credit unions as a 'good thing' deserving of their
support. The chief disadvantage of the credit union, of course, was the
relatively low rate of return on your investment. This (and other
disadvantages of the credit union) was mentioned with increasing
frequency the higher up the income scale people were.

For people with relatively large incomes and high savings
potential, the credit union seems to have had a rather limited appeal,
compared with the wide range of alternative institutions competing for

**Table 4.4** **Advantages and disadvantages of saving with a credit union, by available family income**

*Percentages of member-families*

| Available family income | Total | Under £10 pw | £10 to £49 | £50 to £109 | £110 or more |
|---|---|---|---|---|---|
| **Advantages** | | | | | |
| Convenience | 39 | 42 | 52 | 42 | 19 |
| Opportunity to borrow | 45 | 43 | 46 | 38 | 53 |
| CU good in principle | 16 | 6 | 21 | 14 | 24 |
| Various other advantages | 17 | 15 | 9 | 25 | 18 |
| No advantages | 8 | 9 | 5 | 7 | 10 |
| **Disadvantages** | | | | | |
| Lack of/low dividend | 23 | 8 | 22 | 31 | 30 |
| Inconvenience | 8 | 4 | 4 | 9 | 13 |
| Various other disadvantages | 14 | 7 | 19 | 14 | 25 |
| No disadvantages | 53 | 79 | 49 | 46 | 39 |
| (Sample size) | (231) | (55) | (59) | (59) | (57) |

Note:   Answers to these questions were recorded in full and summarised in the office. Totals add to more than 100% because each respondent could list more than one advantage or disadvantage.

their business. For families with lower incomes, on the other hand, the credit union was seen to be a convenient method of saving, without many drawbacks.

## Savings with the credit union

Leaders of the credit union movement emphasised the ideal of the participating member as someone who made a regular weekly (or monthly) contribution to savings. This increased the member's shareholding, and with it his or her options for taking out a loan; it also built up the union's stock of capital out of which to offer loans. Regular savings were encouraged by the arrangements for collecting payments.   The workplace credit union (Borough) deducted all payments direct from wages and salaries.  About half the members of two unions said that payments were collected from their own home (though neither of these unions had told the researcher that such a service was available, and the finding is therefore unclear). But the great majority of credit union members took their regular instalments to a collection point in person. With the exception of the largest union (N. Ireland, with its permanently staffed premises), collecting sessions were organised one evening a week and were considered to provide a strong social focus for the membership.

But only about two-thirds of members (70 per cent) were making regular payments into their savings/share accounts at the time of their interview. Many of the others had made regular payments in the past, or paid in money from time to time, or at least had some money in their account, but they nevertheless form a core of members not contributing regularly into the pool. Most of the non-savers were not repaying a loan either, and therefore can be said to be sleeping members of their unions. At the Borough union, where payments were deducted from earnings at source, all but 6 per cent were regular savers, and this is evidently an effective way of encouraging good discipline among members. But the proportion of non-regular savers

**Chart 4.5    Proportion of members making regular weekly savings**

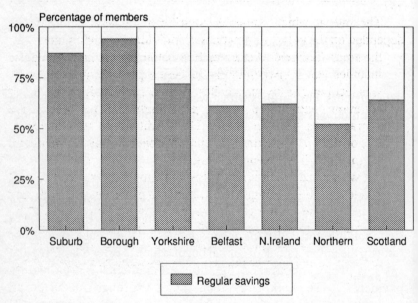

ranged between 13 per cent and 48 per cent at the other six unions covered by the survey (Chart 4.5); on the whole the richer unions were more successful at encouraging regular payments than the poorer ones.

Table 4.6 shows that regular contributions were most common among members with large resources of savings elsewhere; they were least common for people with very low independent savings. But people with no outside savings at all were quite likely to be making regular payments; this group may include people who had decided to transfer the whole of their savings activity to the credit union.

**Table 4.6    Regular contributions to credit union savings, by level of outside savings**

|  | | | *Percentage of members* |
|---|---|---|---|
| **Outside savings** | None at all | Up to £200 | £201 to £1000 | More than £1000 |
| Makes regular contributions | 74 | 44 | 69 | 85 |
| (Sample size) | (94) | (38) | (54) | (44) |

The rate at which members contributed towards their savings depended on the policy or practices of individual credit unions:

* the union (Suburb) whose members had much the highest regular incomes, and overwhelmingly the largest pool of outside savings, was receiving easily the smallest regular contributions. The most common contribution was £1 per month (23p per week); the average was 80p per week. The credit union was therefore responsible for an extremely minor proportion of its members' savings-and-investment package.
* the workplace credit union (Borough), in contrast, used payroll deductions to encourage a much higher rate of savings. Hardly any members paid as little as £3 per week, and the average was £12.30.
* four unions (Yorkshire, N. Ireland, Northern and Scotland) fell between these extremes. Regular subscriptions often lay in the range of £1 to £3 per week; their averages were between £1.90 and £3.30.

**Chart 4.7    Average rates of regular savings payments, by union**

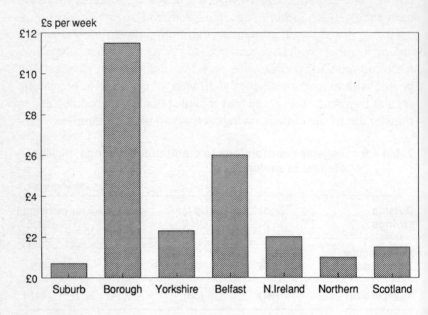

Note:    Chart confined to members who reported regular savings

- but Belfast's most common subscriptions were in the £5 to £10 per week range. Its average was £10.30. But there is no indication of a reason why this union should be different from the other four just described.

The variation between unions is illustrated in Chart 4.7.

These differences are clearly caused by the policies of each union. They could not be simply the natural pattern of contributions offered by the people who happen to be members. Because of the influence of the individual unions, it is difficult to use the survey to work out what other aspects of people's circumstances help to decide the rate at which they save. But if we look only at the four unions with similar average contributions, the signs are that better-off members contributed at a higher rate than poorer ones (Table 4.8).

These regular savings build up to form credit unions' capital base. In each of the unions studied, there was a clear link between individual members' total shareholding and the length of time since they had

**Table 4.8    Average weekly rates of regular savings, by available family income**

*Pounds per week*

| Available family income | Less than £10 pw | £10 to £49 | £50 to £109 | £110 or more |
|---|---|---|---|---|
| Average payment | £1.80 | £2.40 | £3.50 | £4.30 |
| (Sample size) | (29) | (21) | (20) | (11) |

Note:    Table based on those members of the Yorkshire, N. Ireland, Northern and Scotland credit unions who made regular savings payments.

joined. This meant that the oldest union (N. Ireland) had easily the largest average shareholding and the other long-established union (Suburb) had a much larger stock of capital than its very low rate of contributions might have led one to suppose. Looking at savings from the point of view of individual members, however, it is more appropriate to express their shareholdings in terms of how much they had built up for each year since they joined. Looked at in this way, Suburb and Borough stood out as having the slowest and fastest rates of savings accumulation, and this was consistent with their contribution rates (Chart 4.9). On the other hand Belfast's high contributions did not seem to be reflected in rapid accumulation of assets, and it may suffer high rates of withdrawal. The Northern union's savings pool was growing pretty slowly, partly because of relatively small contributions, and partly because many members were not contributing at all. It was doing significantly worse in this respect than the Scotland union, whose members were at least as poor.

The details of each union's savings pattern may be of direct interest mainly to the leaders of those unions. The point of general interest is the range of the variation between them. To a certain extent it may be up to each union to determine the rate of accumulation it wants to aim for. Suburb and Borough appear to have taken decisions leading to relatively small and large savings respectively. On the other hand, Belfast's attempt to build up its pool quickly does not seem to have paid off. And Northern's performance (so far – it is the most recently established of these groups) is disappointing.

These big differences between unions and between long- and short-term members make it rather difficult to show what other factors

**Chart 4.9    Annual accumulation of savings, by union**

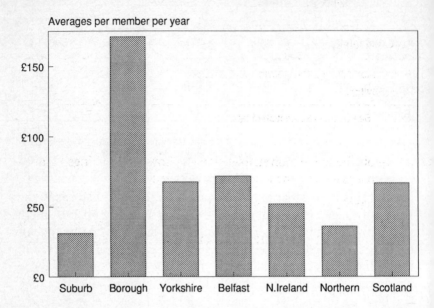

Averages per member per year

Note:    The chart excludes members who joined during the same year as they were
interviewed.

affect savings, and how credit union savings compare with savings in
building societies and other institutions, discussed earlier in this
chapter. Table 4.10 has been calculated in the following way:

- the table excludes members of Suburb and Borough, because their
  savings were so heavily influenced by the union's policy;
- the table also excludes people who had joined during the same year
  as they were interviewed, because 'savings per year' were so
  difficult to calculate;
- savings-per-year were multiplied by six to make an estimate of
  savings-per-six-years; this gives a better impression of the actual
  level of savings people had accumulated, because they had
  belonged to a union for about six years on average.
- the credit union savings of husbands and wives were added
  together, to make them comparable with the family's savings
  elsewhere;
- a calculation was made of the relationship between family income
  and the family's level of savings inside and outside the credit

**Table 4.10  Credit union and other savings, by available family income**

| | | | Regression points |
|---|---|---|---|
| **Available family income** | £10 | £60 | £110 |
| Credit union savings (six years) | £300 | £380 | £460 |
| Other savings | £120 | £380 | £640 |

Note:    See text for explanation of table.

union; the calculation enabled us to say how much savings a family with a given income tended to have saved.

This table says that a typical family with an income £10 above the supplementary benefit level had accumulated an average of £300 in the union after six years; the same family also had an average of £120 saved in a building society or bank. A second family, earning £100 more than the first, typically had about £460 in the credit union, and £640 elsewhere. Thus well-off people were contributing more to the union than their poorer neighbours. But it was shown earlier that people with relatively low incomes had a more favourable impression of the credit union, compared with a building society; it is now clear that the poorer members were placing a much higher proportion of their limited savings with their credit union.

# 5. Members' Use of Credit

Although many members thought that the opportunity to save was at least as important as the credit facility, the direct link between savings and loans is the distinctive feature of a credit union. As in the previous chapter, members' activities in the general market place are considered before their use of the credit union.

### Credit from other sources

A few years ago, the National Consumer Council commissioned a survey about people's attitudes to and use of credit. An important question from that survey was repeated in the current survey of credit union members. Table 5.1 compares the results of the two surveys,

**Table 5.1 Attitude to buying on credit: credit union members compared with general population**

*Percentage of members*

|  | Credit union members | General population |
|---|---|---|
| Never a good thing | 16 | 21 |
| Occasionally necessary | 55 | 47 |
| Convenient way of buying | 19 | 23 |
| Sensible way of buying | 8 | 5 |
| (Don't know) | (2) | (4) |
| (Sample size) | (205) | (910) |

Notes: 1. Figures for general population from NCC survey on *Consumers and Credit*.
2. Both sets of figures confined to respondents below pension age.

and shows that credit union members took broadly the same view as other people – as a group, they were neither particularly pro nor particularly anti credit. (The one exception was among the members of the N. Ireland credit union, where half of those interviewed said that credit was 'never a good thing'.)

The people in the current survey were, however, bound to be different from the rest of the population in one respect: they had access to credit union loans. The fact that the interview was specifically about the credit union would have brought this to the front of their minds. Even so, when they were asked to say what kinds of credit they preferred to use, and what types they would rather not use, credit union loans came out miles ahead of the rest of the field (Table 5.2). Only one other source of credit – the mail order catalogue – was preferred by more people than rejected it. Other sources were viewed with doubt, and others – trading checks, finance company loans, door to door salesmen and money lenders and pawnbrokers – were highly unpopular.

**Table 5.2    Attitudes to different sources of credit**

*Percentage of members*

| | Prefer to use | Rather not use | Net preference |
|---|---|---|---|
| Credit union loan | 86 | 1 | +85 |
| Mail order catalogue | 26 | 15 | +11 |
| Electricity/gas board credit | 8 | 15 | -7 |
| Bank loan | 12 | 20 | -8 |
| Store credit account | 11 | 21 | -10 |
| Building society loan | 7 | 18 | -11 |
| Access/Barclaycard | 17 | 33 | -16 |
| Hire purchase | 14 | 37 | -23 |
| Check or voucher trading | 1 | 34 | -33 |
| Finance company loan | * | 40 | -40 |
| Door to door salesman | * | 61 | -61 |
| Moneylender/pawnbroker | nil | 78 | -78 |
| (Sample size) | (231) | (231) | |

Notes:    The third column is calculated by subtracting the second from the first.
      * = less than 0.5%.

Even though credit union loans were more popular than other types of credit, the majority of members had used at least one type of alternative source within the past year. This might mean arranging credit at the time of buying something (eg buying in instalments from a mail order catalogue, hire purchase) or arranging credit with a financial institution prior to purchasing goods or services (eg a credit card or a bank loan). Table 5.3 combines both credit purchases and loans to show the extent to which members of different social groups used different sources. People in professional and managerial occupations commonly used credit cards, bank loans or store accounts; the clerical group used mail order, credit cards and bank loans; but manual workers used few sources of credit other than the mail order catalogue; and people without employment appeared to be even more restricted to mail order. Some of them had even resorted to check trading, one of the most unpopular methods.

**Table 5.3   Uses of different sources of non-union credit in past year, by occupational group**

*Percentage of member-families*

| Occupational group | Total | Professionals/ managers | Clerical | Manual workers | Non-workers |
|---|---|---|---|---|---|
| Mail order catalogue | 36 | 11 | 54 | 39 | 35 |
| Credit card | 23 | 63 | 47 | 13 | 3 |
| Bank loan | 15 | 36 | 24 | 14 | 1 |
| Store credit account | 13 | 33 | 10 | 13 | 5 |
| Hire purchase | 11 | 13 | 2 | 16 | 8 |
| Check or voucher trading | 8 | nil | 4 | 6 | 16 |
| Elec/gas board credit | 7 | 3 | 10 | 9 | 4 |
| Building society loan | 2 | 8 | 1 | 2 | nil |
| Finance company loan | 2 | 2 | 3 | 2 | nil |
| Door to door salesman | nil | nil | nil | nil | nil |
| Moneylender/ pawnbroker | nil | nil | nil | nil | nil |
| Total of these items | 117 | 169 | 165 | 117 | 72 |
| (Sample size) | (231) | (36) | (37) | (84) | (74) |

Note:   Items are listed in order of their frequency of use.

It is important to try to assess how credit union members' behaviour in the 'open market' compares with that of ordinary families who have not joined a union. Table 5.4 makes this comparison for low and high income families, based on a survey carried out for the Office of Fair Trading carried out at about the same time as our own. The comparison is not based on identical questions or exactly equivalent samples, so it is not precise. The signs are that:
- the use of credit cards is slightly lower among union members than among the population at large;
- credit union members have a higher than average use of the other four main credit sources, at least in the middle and upper income ranges.

**Table 5.4   Use of non-union sources of credit by gross family income: credit union members compared with all families**

*Percentages*

|  | at £5,000 per year | | at £15,000 per year | |
|  | All families | CU members | All families | CU members |
|---|---|---|---|---|
| Credit card | 20 | 13 | 47 | 43 |
| Loans | 10 | 9 | 25 | 34 |
| Store credit | 6 | 7 | 16 | 21 |
| Hire purchase etc | 7 | 12 | 14 | 23 |
| Mail order instalments | 35 | 39 | 13 | 20 |

Notes:   1. Data for all families based on a question on types of credit 'used nowadays' in PAS *Consumer Credit Survey* 1988.
2. The table shows estimates (using simple regression equations) of the rate of use of each source of credit for families with a gross income of £5,000 or of £15,000 per year.

The evidence is by no means conclusive, but there is little sign that a credit union is a substitute for other types of credit. On the contrary, it looks like a useful expansion of the range of credit sources available to middle income families.

Returning to the survey of union members, the average credit transaction (ie credit purchase or loan, excluding credit union loans) involved £440. But this average covers a very wide range of sums:

| | |
|---|---|
| Up to £25 | 10 per cent of transactions |
| £26 to £50 | 13 per cent |
| £50 to £100 | 18 per cent |
| £101 to £250 | 17 per cent |
| £251 to £500 | 13 per cent |
| £501 to £1000 | 17 per cent |
| Over £1000 | 14 per cent |

A variety of things had been bought on credit:

| | |
|---|---|
| Clothes and shoes | 27 per cent of transactions |
| Household equipment | 21 per cent |
| Leisure items | 8 per cent |
| Vehicles | 5 per cent |
| Repairs and decoration | 5 per cent |
| Travel and holidays | 5 per cent |
| Weddings, Christmas etc | 3 per cent |
| Mixed items, other items | 25 per cent |

But, as might have been expected, large and small purchases were often financed by different sources of credit (Table 5.5). Thus vehicles tended to have been bought with the aid of bank loans or hire purchase agreements; household appliances on HP or on the supplier's own credit scheme; clothing was often bought on a store scheme, or by mail order. Credit cards tended to have been used to buy a variety of items, probably from different retailers.

**Table 5.5    Details of non-union credit transactions, by type of credit used[1]**

| Type of credit | Bank loan | Hire purchase | Credit card | Supplier | Mail order |
|---|---|---|---|---|---|
| Average amount | £1150 | £910 | £340 | £160 | £90 |
| Main purposes[2] | Vehicles | Appliances Vehicles | Mixed | Clothing Appliances | Clothing |

Notes:   1. Types of credit are listed in order of the average amount. 'Supplier' includes store accounts and fuel boards. 33 transactions using a variety of other sources of credit have been omitted from the table.
2. The table specifies all purposes accounting for a quarter or more of the transactions of each type.

More than two thirds of all families belonging to a credit union reported some non-union credit transactions over the past year. Adding up all such transactions, the average non-union credit user had borrowed £710 over the year. The same figure averaged over all member-families (including those who did not borrow) comes to £500.*

Table 5.3 compared access to and use of different sources of credit of members of different occupational groups. Table 5.6 shows the variation in the total amount borrowed from non-union institutions.

**Table 5.6   Extent of use of non-union credit, by occupational group**

*Percentage of member-families*

| Occupational group | Total | Professionals/ managers | Clerical | Manual workers | Non-working |
|---|---|---|---|---|---|
| Percent use any credit | 70% | 90% | 89% | 66% | 55% |
| Average amount (users) | £710 | £1,240 | £670 | £720 | £290 |
| Average amount (all) | £500 | £1,110 | £600 | £480 | £160 |
| (Sample size) | (231) | (36) | (37) | (84) | (74) |

Middle class people were most likely to borrow elsewhere, and borrowed more if they did; non-working families were much less likely to use outside credit, and did so on a smaller scale. The combined effect of the frequency and size of credit transactions adds up to a huge difference in the use of non-union sources: the professional/ managerial families were seven times as active in the market as the non-working families.

The NCC survey of the use of credit already referred to suggested that non-working families (other than pensioners) were just as likely to have used credit as middle class families were, although they did

---

* The question about non-union credit transactions will tend to understate the annual total of forms of credit (like mail order or credit cards) used regularly. The average of £500 per family will therefore be an underestimate.

so on a smaller scale. Among credit union members, manual workers and non-workers were relatively unlikely to operate in the wider market. This might mean that the credit union has succeeded in replacing outside sources of credit for the lower-ranking occupational groups, to a greater extent than among those at the top of the hierarchy.

Other important influences on union members' use of credit also reflected the national picture shown by the NCC survey: families with children and young people used more credit than people without children or older people (Table 5.7).

**Table 5.7  Extent of use of non-union credit by family structure and age**

*Member-families*

| Family structure | With children | Without children | Non-householder |
|---|---|---|---|
| Average amount (all) | £660 | £350 | £380 |

| Age | Up to 34 | 35 to 49 | 50 or over |
|---|---|---|---|
| Average amount (all) | £570 | £590 | £350 |

## Loans from the credit union
### Size and purpose of loans

More than half (58 per cent) of the families in the sample had borrowed from their credit union during the past year. This is far more than had used any other particular type of credit – the next most common, mail order, had been used by about one third. If we consider all other types of credit together, however, rather more had borrowed outside the union than had used the union itself.

Three-quarters of members (or their spouses) had taken out a credit union loan at some time (if not in the past year, then previously). Analysis of the last loan reported by each member of the sample gave an average amount borrowed of £440. Credit union loans therefore tended to be smaller than the bank loans and hire purchase transactions reported by union members, but larger than credit card accounts, credit arranged at the point of sale or mail order transactions (Table 5.8).

**Table 5.8    Sizes of credit union and non-CU advances**

*Percentages of transactions*

|  | Credit union loans | Other loans | Credit purchases |
|---|---|---|---|
| Up to £25 | 2 | nil | 11 |
| £26 to £50 | 3 | 2 | 15 |
| £51 to £100 | 6 | 9 | 21 |
| £101 to £250 | 31 | 15 | 20 |
| £251 to £500 | 25 | 13 | 23 |
| £501 to £1,000 | 19 | 16 | 6 |
| More than £1,000 | 14 | 45 | 4 |
| Average | £440 | £1,080 | £260 |
| (Sample size) | (179) | (57) | (204) |

**Table 5.9    Purpose of credit union and non-CU advances**

*Percentages of transactions*

|  | Credit union loans | Other loans | Credit purchases |
|---|---|---|---|
| Travel and holidays | 17 | 6 | 5 |
| Vehicles | 14 | 16 | 3 |
| Weddings, Christmas etc | 11 | 11 | 2 |
| To pay bills | 11 | 4 | nil |
| Repairs and decoration | 9 | 16 | 1 |
| Household goods | 8 | 3 | 26 |
| Clothes and shoes | 8 | 10 | 31 |
| To repay other loans or debts | 6 | 16 | nil |
| Leisure items | 4 | 3 | 10 |
| Mixed items, other items | 17 | 14 | 23 |
| (Sample size) | (179) | (57) | (204) |

Table 5.9 shows that 'credit purchases' were concentrated on clothing and household goods, both of which are commonly sold on credit terms at the point of sale or by mail order. But non-union loans covered a much wider range. Credit union loans were similar to non-union cash loans in the variety of expenses they were used to pay for.

One difference between a credit union and other financial institutions is that it is quite normal for a member to have both savings and a loan at the same time. People are not expected to withdraw their savings if they need cash – indeed they are encouraged not to. They take out a loan instead. It is therefore appropriate to compare members' loans with their savings to get an impression of their net balance. The information available does not provide this very precisely: we know the level of savings of the member (and his or her spouse) at the time of the interview, and compare this with the size of the last loan taken out by the member (or his/her spouse) within the past year (Table 5.10).

As a broad rule, member-families with high levels of savings tended to take out larger loans than those with lower savings. There is a whole series of reasons why this should happen. First, unions whose members have collectively built up large pools of savings were in a position to offer large loans. Second, individuals with large savings would be seen both as loyal members and as good risks, and loan committees would encourage them to make use of the union's credit services. Third, families with high incomes would tend both to build

**Table 5.10 Comparison of credit union loans with credit union savings**

| | | | *Percentage of member families* |
|---|---|---|---|
| **Family savings** | Up to £50 | £51 to £500 | £501 or more |
| **Last loan** | | | |
| Up to £100 | 40 | 5 | 4 |
| £101 to £500 | 58 | 68 | 32 |
| £501 or more | 2 | 27 | 64 |
| Average | £160 | £380 | £750 |
| (Sample size) | (24) | (93) | (46) |

up savings more quickly than than their poorer fellow members, and would also want to borrow in larger amounts. For all these reasons, there is a natural tendency for credit unions' capital to be recycled as loans to broadly the same people as provided it in the first place.

There was no real difference between better-off and worse-off families, in the number of loans they drew from their unions. The average for all income groups was about one loan every 41 weeks. But the size of each loan was directly related to the family income, so that the top income group tended to borrow three times as much as the bottom group (Table 5.11). This might be either because low-income families tended to prefer relatively modest sums, or because either they or the credit union leaders felt that they ought not to overstretch their commitments beyond their ability to repay.

**Table 5.11  Size of credit union loans, by available family income**

*Percentage of member - families*

| Available family income | Less than £10 pw | £10 to £49 | £50 to £109 | £110 or more |
|---|---|---|---|---|
| Up to £100 | 24 | 14 | 6 | nil |
| £101 to £250 | 41 | 47 | 22 | 19 |
| £251 to £500 | 23 | 17 | 37 | 22 |
| £501 to £1,000 | 12 | 14 | 19 | 29 |
| £1,001 or more | nil | 8 | 16 | 30 |
| Average | £220 | £330 | £490 | £680 |
| (Sample size) | (43) | (40) | (51) | (46) |

Note:   'Available income' is calculated as the difference between the family's net income and the supplementary benefit scale rate.

Table 5.12 compares the use of credit union loans with access to money from non-union sources. It can be seen that the difference between income groups is similar for both types of credit. Credit unions therefore appear to reflect the pattern of credit use available to people in different circumstances, rather than transform it.

**Table 5.12  Union and non-union credit, by available family income**

*Member - families*

| Available family income | Less than £10 pw | £10 to £49 | £50 to £109 | £110 or more |
|---|---|---|---|---|
| Credit union loans per year | £160 | £230 | £390 | £440 |
| Non-union credit last year | £260 | £310 | £530 | £890 |
| Total | £420 | £540 | £920 | £1320 |
| Credit union as % of total | 38% | 43% | 42% | 33% |
| (Sample size) | (55) | (59) | (59) | (59) |

Note:    'Available income' is calculated as the difference between the family's net income and the supplementary benefitscale rate.

### *Procedure for obtaining credit union loans*

When people who had taken out a credit union loan were asked how they had gone about applying for it, there were enormous differences between the unions in the aspects of the procedure which members were most conscious of. At some unions, they thought about the place they went to to discuss a loan. At others they tended to think about the paperwork. At some unions, borrowers talked about the people through which the application was processed. We can draw no conclusion about the pattern of variations between unions, other than that members' view of the procedure is highly localised.

A third (35 per cent) of members who had taken out a loan said that they had been interviewed in person by the loan committee. This happened nearly nine times out of ten for loans provided by the two poorest unions.  All the other unions' loan committees appeared to interview some applicants in person, but this was only a minority. Those who had been interviewed were asked to comment on the experience: most did so in favourable or neutral terms, and only a few felt that it had been intrusive or embarrassing.

Other procedures were adopted in particular by different unions. The N. Ireland credit union had a staff of full-time workers, and about half of its loans were cleared in the office. All the other unions had relied on officers to deal with a minority of their transactions. Members of the Yorkshire union commonly mentioned friends or relatives as the people who had dealt with their application, and this suggests a grapevine of negotiations.

Only a handful of union members said they had ever applied for a loan and been turned down – except at N. Ireland, where a quarter of all members had been rejected at one stage or another of their (long) period of membership. Only a handful of those who succeeded in obtaining a loan were lent less than they had asked to borrow. Only a handful were asked to obtain the consent of another member of the union to guarantee repayment – except at Yorkshire, where a third of all loans had to be backed by a guarantor. The great majority of people said they were 'very' happy with the way their loan application had been dealt with. There were two exceptions: the few who had been rejected were naturally unhappy about it; and members of the Borough credit union mostly said that they were only 'fairly' happy about the loans procedure. It was seen in Chapter 3 that members of this work-based union showed evidence of relatively poor morale, and this grudging appreciation of the loans system is further evidence of it.

One way of finding out what role credit union loans played in their members' budget management was to ask people what they would have done if they had not obtained their latest loan:

| | |
|---|---|
| Would have borrowed money elsewhere | 32 per cent |
| Would not have bought items | 26 per cent |
| Would have drawn out CU savings | 17 per cent |
| Would have drawn out other savings | 12 per cent |
| Would have paid cash | 7 per cent |
| Would have bought on credit | 4 per cent |

## Repayment arrangements

Once a member had taken out a loan, it was repaid in instalments by the same method as was used for paying in savings contributions: most often paid in person to the union, usually at a weekly collection session; for the work-based union, by deduction from earnings.

The great majority of loan repayment instalments were in the range between £2 and £15 per week (or monthly equivalents). The average was £9.10. This varied between about £3 per week at Northern and nearly £12 per week at Suburb, Borough and N. Ireland. The principal influence on the size of repayment instalments, however, was the size of the loan (Table 5.13) and there was little difference between unions once the variations in the average size of loan is taken into account.

**Table 5.13  Repayment instalments, by size of loan**

| Size of loan | Up to £100 | £101 to £250 | £251 to £500 | £501 to £1000 | £1001 or more |
|---|---|---|---|---|---|
| Up to £2.00 | 25 | 3 | nil | nil | nil |
| £2.01 - £5.00 | 45 | 44 | 8 | 7 | 4 |
| £5.01 - £10.00 | 21 | 36 | 53 | 36 | nil |
| £10.01 - £15.00 | 8 | 13 | 32 | 21 | 30 |
| £15.01 or more | nil | 4 | 8 | 46 | 65 |
| Average | £3.30 | £5.40 | £8.20 | £12.80 | £18.80 |
| Sample size | (19) | (55) | (38) | (32) | (23) |

Note:    Table confined to loans whose repayment details were known.

There was a big gap between the repayment instalments paid by people with relatively high or low incomes: those with an available income of less than £10 per week paid only £5.30 for their loans on average, while those with more than £110 of available income paid £12.40. But this difference was almost entirely due to the fact that better-off people tended to take out larger loans. We calculate that if a member of the richest group and of the poorest group both took out the same loans, the difference in their instalments would be only about £1.50 per week. It is commonly said that credit unions ask their members to repay loans at a rate linked to what they can afford. This is true only to the extent that the loans themselves are related to what members can afford to pay back; the rate of repayment of any particular loan is only weakly influenced by the borrower's circumstances.

Union leaders and the analysis of annual accounts in Chapter 1 have told us that interest on credit union loans is almost always charged at a rate of 1 per cent per month. It was notable that three-fifths of those who had borrowed from the union were unable to provide any indication of the rate of interest they paid. Even among those who gave an answer, there was confusion, including some wrong answers and others stated in terms of pence per week. But 60 per cent could not even guess, and cannot have 'shopped around' for the best interest rate available. As one might have expected, members of professional and managerial occupations commonly had some idea about this (68 per cent), but manual workers and non-workers did not (32 per cent).

Assuming 1 per cent per month, the average loan of £440 repaid at £9.10 per week would take just under a year to clear – 51 weeks. Comparison between loans of different sizes showed a compromise between the rate of repayment and the duration of the loan: larger loans were scheduled both to have larger instalments and to take longer to repay. This is best illustrated by showing how some typical loans would be repaid (Table 5.14).

**Table 5.14  Average repayment programmes for loans of different sizes**

| Size of loan | £100 | £500 | £1000 |
|---|---|---|---|
| **Available income £10** | | | |
| Weekly rate | £4.80 | £9.50 | £15.30 |
| No. of weeks | 21 | 56 | 71 |
| **Available income £110** | | | |
| Weekly rate | £5.60 | £10.30 | £16.10 |
| No. of weeks | 18 | 51 | 67 |

Note:  Estimates derived from regression equation:
Weekly payments = 0.0117 x Size of loan
+ 0.00825 x Available income
+ 3.51

# 6. Problems with Repayments

One of the drawbacks of using credit, especially by families on low incomes, is the risk of falling into difficulties with repayments. Concern is often expressed at the number of people facing court procedures or other sanctions for the recovery of debt. Leaders of the credit union movement are keen to help protect their members from indebtedness in three ways: first, by offering credit at cheaper rates than may be available elsewhere, especially from money-lenders; second by limiting advances to what the individual can afford to repay; third, by ensuring that any difficulties over repayment are dealt with in a sensitive way.

Although credit unions intend to avoid the problems of debt, it is nevertheless possible for members to fall behind with their repayment instalments. This chapter examines the evidence on repayment arrears from all three of the main sources: the survey of members; the analysis of annual accounts; and the interviews with officers and committees.

### Members' experiences and attitudes
The great majority of the members who had ever taken out a loan from their union said that they had never had any problems finding the money. But 13 per cent of borrowers said that they had missed payments at some time. At least one member of every union reported some repayment difficulties, with the exception of the employment-based union (Borough) which arranged for repayment instalments to be paid out of wages. About half of those with any problem said they had missed only one or two payments, but the other half had missed several. Among these a handful – four members of the sample – gave an indication that their difficulties had been serious. This is a very

small minority, but it is not possible to say with any certainty whether problems over credit union repayments are any less common than arrears on other kinds of loan. Unfortunately, but not unexpectedly, most of the people who reported repayment problems had low incomes (Table 6.1).

**Table 6.1    Difficulties with repayment, by available family income**

*Percentage of members*

| Available family income | Less than £10 pw | £10 to £49 | £50 to £109 | £110 or more |
|---|---|---|---|---|
| Had missed payments on credit union loans | 30 | 8 | 5 | 8 |
| (Sample size) | (43) | (40) | (51) | (46) |

Note:    Table confined to members who had ever had a loan.

It is likely that any member who had completely defaulted on a loan would have been expected to resign from his or her credit union, and would therefore not have been included in the sample of people interviewed. Even so, it was notable what a relaxed attitude people had towards the procedures which took effect when instalments were missed. When those who had missed payments were asked what had happened, the most common single answer was 'nothing' – that is, they had returned to steady payments without a fuss being made on either side. Others said that the officers had written to them to ask about the missed payments. Some had got in touch with the union to explain their difficulty.

> I went down and explained the situation to the people in the office who sorted things out and brought payments down by half.

> (I had) one missed payment due to problems with my pension. The credit union didn't bother. (I) just paid double next week.

Similarly, most people who had not experienced repayment problems assumed that the credit union would get in touch with slow payers to find out what the problem was. Many thought that it would be possible for borrowers to pay at a reduced rate, or pay interest only for a while, until they were in a better position to pay up. Only six members suggested that the credit union would take people to court to collect arrears. More than a third simply had no idea what would happen if they fell behind.

> Maybe someone would come to see you, check whether you were sick or what was wrong.

> I'd get a reminder letter and then they'd arrange for someone to see me and arrange for me to pay less, pay what I could afford.

> I don't know, I think they would wait until I could afford it.

## Bad debts

The annual accounts submitted by credit unions to the Registrars of Friendly Societies include a statement of bad debts written off, though it is difficult to draw conclusions about bad debts from the items recorded in a single year. It is not possible to determine whether a low bad debt figure means that the credit union has a generally good record of securing repayment; has done better this year than it expected to last year; or has been over-optimistic in its allowance for losses. High figures are equally hard to interpret. It is, however, possible to assess average figures for a group of credit unions with more confidence.

Figures in Chapter 1 show that the average credit union in Northern Ireland allowed for a loss of £5,080 of bad and doubtful debts in 1986 (£6,380 written off; £1,300 recovered). This is 10 per cent of the income derived from the interest paid on loans. Another way of putting it is that the effective rate of return on loans is reduced from 12.7 per cent to 11.4 per cent.

Only five Northern Ireland credit unions felt confident enough to record zero bad debts in 1986. On the other hand, none recorded bad debts in excess of a third of the interest payable. There was little sign that larger or smaller, richer or poorer, stable or growing unions were particularly at risk of bad debts.

Bad and doubtful debts reported in Great Britain averaged £540 per union, representing 9 per cent of loan interest. This was a slightly better performance than in Northern Ireland, where the equivalent figure was 10 per cent. But it is notable that half of the British unions made no provision at all for bad debts in their latest returns. Less than a quarter of the smallest British unions made any provison, though the figure rose to 90 per cent among the larger groups. A zero allocation indicates either a very healthy repayment rate, or rather imprudent accountancy practices.

At the other extreme, five unions in Great Britain wrote off more than half of their income from loan interest against bad or doubtful debts in their latest accounts. At least one of these is known to have improved its debt recovery since then, but some of the others may be in trouble.

## Leaders' assessment of the problem

The officers and committee members of the 12 credit unions investigated in detail varied in the extent to which they were having to deal with arrears. One union had never had any 'delinquent accounts'; another 'very few'. Other groups felt that it was a major problem – the most serious problem they had had to deal with. Arrears and bad debts diminished the pool of savings available to lend to members, and reduced the income needed to build up reserves and pay a dividend. These problems might then discourage members from saving with the union, and the vicious circle of financial difficulties and lowered morale might eventually threaten a credit union with bankruptcy. So ensuring prompt and regular repayments was one of the major responsibilities of the leadership group.

> We were inexperienced in lending and got involved in some bad debts which weren't paid back. We had to put a lot into reserve to build up against it and therefore we couldn't pay the dividend that was expected ... I think a lot of people felt 'Well, we might as well put our money in the bank or somewhere else.' The dividend is quite a good part of it all, people think ... We saw ... the dividend being nil, nil, nil, year after year. The penny dropped that something really had to be done to set up a system for credit control and one could no longer just depend on this trust. People were just taking advantage.

> The unemployment started. It grew and delinquency grew as well. There would not have been delinquency otherwise. The black people in the credit union were more at risk from unemployment. Until 1978 it was quite stable because everybody had a job and was quite motivated. It still appeared stable several years after that, but it was actually declining while we were not aware of the real situation. Delinquency grew and more and more energies should have been put into dealing with it at the time. Because they were not, it is haunting us now. It had grown into a very large problem by the time we tried to tackle it.

Leaders' comments on these problems indicated that there were two types of influence on the extent of the problem. One lay in the membership and the strength of the common bond. The other lay in the union's policy and procedures for giving loans and chasing up repayments.

### Membership

The two unions with the least problem of this sort both recruited their members from among relatively prosperous middle-income families, and this may be a sufficient explanation for their good payment record. On the other hand, the leaders attributed their success to the fact that they had restricted membership to a small tight-knit group of people, mostly members of their local Catholic Church. Indeed the whole point of credit unions is that group membership and loyalties should substitute for other forms of sanction in encouraging full and prompt repayment of loans.

It was therefore considered important that members and officers should know each other, and that these connections should regularly be reinforced by contact at collections and at other types of meeting. This policy was much more difficult to achieve if the number of members was large, or if the common bond was one which did not inspire strong loyalties: residence in a particular area, or working for an employer.

> Those people who were members in those days, who live far away ... we do not even know their faces and they are the ones that have quite a lot of delinquent amounts out. If we were in a community where we were moving amongst one another we would have seen them and better contact would be made.

> The boundary is sort of a protection so your members are all together. If you do incur any bad debts, you don't have to chase all over town looking for them. We found that the majority of bad debts came from outside our common bond. So we keep that as strict now. They have to live in the area. Delinquency hasn't been as rampant.

These considerations suggested a policy of confining membership to people who were clearly within the common bond. Indeed, one officer suggested that there might even be a common bond of disloyalty among people on the fringes.

> You do find that you get groups of members who joined about the same time from the same area, quite close. Those are people who never really had any intention. They start quite well and have a first loan, pay some of it off and then go for as much as they can

get, husband and wife and maybe some of the family. There's a
very small percentage like that.

A union could face problems if it tried to expand its membership by
recruiting outside its original core group. For example, a credit union
formed among the people in one division of an employer's workforce
decided to take members from other divisions:

They weren't just in a different building, they were actually not
even doing the same sort of work as us ... We had great difficulties
in communicating with them and that in turn led to delinquent loans
... We didn't have the daily working contact with them that we
have with other people in the same building and therefore couldn't
chase them in quite the same way.

## Lending and enforcement policies
Several credit unions had started with an open lending policy, but later
tempered their idealistic approach.

Three years ago it was whoever came, came. But now we've sewn
it down a bit.

We really started without having much idea of what loan policy
we should have ... We just more or less gave the loans that were
asked ... We all knew each other pretty well ... At the beginning
there were two trends... One was people who wanted to use the
loans to help people who were in difficulty – the Christian attitude.
Then there was another group of people who wanted it to be
business – almost like a commercial bank, applying criteria fairly
strictly ... Somehow we tried to meet these two things together. We
had a man who asked for a loan who was actually in prison because
of arrears of rate s... If we could lend him so many hundred pounds,
he would be able to clear his debt, get out of prison and start earning
again and then be able to pay us back. We anguished over this for
a long time. It really was a kind of test case and in the end we gave
it. It's still not been repaid ... We don't want to do that kind of
thing again ... Gradually the trend has moved towards a more
business-like approach.

All officers hoped to ensure as far as possible that members were
'borrowing wisely' when the initial application for a loan was made:

We don't give out loans willy nilly. We don't want to overburden
people with paying us back. Certainly if they have financial
problems and they're coming to us for a loan to pay off a debt, we
don't want to put extra strains on them in terms of repaying it. A
knowledge of the person and their financial state is important to
us.

Although by law credit unions can sue for repayment in the courts and set off the member's savings against the loan, most unions used these tactics as a last resort. Emphasis was put on early intervention. At either the first or the second missed regular payment all the credit unions (except one) would attempt to contact the member either by letter or by 'a word in their ear' to try to establish what the problem was. This usually led to renewed payments, or a renegotiation of repayment terms until the member was in a better position. And all credit unions exhorted their membership to inform them if there were problems or if they foresaw problems on the horizon, so that they could be dealt with. Letters were sometimes supplemented by personal visits.

> If we can get someone to visit for us it helps to keep the people close to us ... They know that we're in touch with them. They can't get down one week and maybe don't go down for two or three weeks. Then all of a sudden they realise they owe £5 instead of £1 and 'Oh, I haven't got £5 this week, I'll leave it till next week.' But it's accumulating. Once it gets to a certain pitch, they're ashamed and afraid to come down because they don't like to say 'I haven't got it'. They've maybe had to use it for something unexpected. This is where we try to say to them, 'If anything happens, tell us. We can perhaps help you adjust it', or we can say, 'right, leave it for a month, if you pay the interest at least it keeps that going and you're still connected.' I find with a lot of cases, a personal approach is better than the letters.

But, as with loans policy, it might take some time to get the right balance between sensitivity and firmness.

> I think by the very nature of the organisation at the beginning, there was a lot of leniency shown towards people that were slow payers. Perhaps we didn't recognise quickly enough that there was a problem there. They were friends and you thought that, well, they'll come through, and they didn't come through ... After a while we had a problem on our hands and we were too slow to recognise it. It was known as the bank with a heart, and perhaps we had too much heart. We went too much humanitarian. Maybe it was a good thing in one way. It's given us a bit of a problem but probably the good that it did outweighed the problems that we were left with. We can cope with them.

Visits to members' homes were not easy to arrange. It was an embarrassing task requiring great tact. Not every volunteer was prepared to be a debt collector. Costs in terms of time, energy and travelling expenses, particularly where the membership were spread over a wide area, could be high for little reward.

> We keep writing every now and again and he sends us a fiver. Sometimes we motor out there and we come back with another fiver. But it's still hundreds of pounds and the interest keeps mounting up.

So although personal contact was really preferred, many credit unions were concentrating their efforts mainly on letter campaigns or phone calls which became increasingly threatening as the weeks passed with no positive response.

All the credit unions tried as far as possible to distinguish between the 'can't pays' and the 'won't pays'. One credit committee said they were dealing with 70 'stutterers' or slow payers – those who paid one week, missed the next two, paid the fourth week and so on. Slow payers were given as much help as possible to improve their repayment record and many were first time loans where members did not fully understand how the credit union worked and the importance of consistent repayments. This could be rectified by an explanation:

> Most delinquent loans are first time loans. People who are on their second or third are better payers. They don't really understand. If they can get help, that's their main interest.

However eight of the twelve credit unions we visited reported a hard core of what one of them called 'vindictive delinquents', who appeared to have no intention of paying up if they could help it. Most of these debts had been pursued by officers for at least six months before being classified as hard core.

In such cases, officers' only recourse was to write the debt off or to make use of the law. Three credit unions said they had never issued summonses although they might have threatened them. Four said they issued three to six per year. The credit union with the largest membership had taken 50 debtors to court in the past eight months. However all agreed that getting a judgement against a member did not necessarily lead to repayment, although it involved the credit union in extra costs which it could ill afford. Most tried to avoid using such extreme measures.

# 7. What Future for Credit Unions?

### The research findings
It is useful to start this concluding chapter with a summary of the research findings reported in earlier chapters.

### *Institutions and finances*
Nearly a third of the adult population of the Republic of Ireland, and a similar proportion of Catholics in Northern Ireland, are members of credit unions. Unions both north and south of the border belong to the Irish League of Credit Unions which has a stable financial base and appears to provide a strong supporting organisation.

The research showed that credit unions in Northern Ireland ranged from 200 to 12,500 members, with an average of more than 1000. Assets had been stable over the past ten years at about £430 per member, and the financial structure did not vary much between larger and smaller unions. Although many of the large groups spent substantial amounts on salaries and accommodation, surpluses were large enough both to pay a dividend on shares and to contribute to reserves. The unions were able to offer loans averaging about £400 each to three-quarters of their members each year.

In England, Wales and Scotland there were three stages of development after the Credit Union Act of 1979: immediate growth; then a pause as several of the new groups got into trouble; and then, recently, a rapid expansion. Credit unions are regulated by the Registrar of Friendly Societies, and belong to one of two umbrella groups. One of the points at issue between the rivals is the relative priority to be given to *instrumental* or *idealistic* considerations in the development of the movement. Credit unions have also been nurtured by specialist development workers, often appointed or supported by local authorities. In spite of the immediate success of some of these initiatives, there is still less than one credit union member for every 1000 members of the adult population.

The average British credit union was much smaller than its counterpart in Northern Ireland, with 280 members. Assets were growing, but were still only £260 per head. Many British unions had low levels of reserves, and could not afford to pay a dividend on shares. They nevertheless managed to offer loans averaging £400 each to three fifths of their members each year. All the indicators showed that the smallest British unions were in the weakest financial position.

### Running a credit union

It was generally argued that the initiative and motivation for starting a credit union should come from the potential members themselves, rather than from outside. It was important to identify a genuine 'common bond', rather than try to create one. In Northern Ireland these bonds were mostly defined in terms of residence or employment within a locality, but there was usually a close link with the Catholic Church. In Great Britain there was a wider range of bonds based on areas of residence, workplaces, churches and other existing associations.

Credit unions belonged to their members, but were administered by a smaller group of elected officers and helpers. Although the work load could be heavy, these leaders were motivated at the same time by a desire to serve their community, and by a combination of more personal considerations. Some of them were elected because of their previous administrative experience; others required training or had to learn as they went along. Many of the leaders were the middle aged, middle class men who often appear to be the 'natural' choices for positions of responsibility, but it was often difficult for the leadership group to recruit others to take their place.

Credit unions often relied heavily on the services of one of the three representative organisations during their early years – for information, training, advice and other administrative services, as well as for insurance. Of the two larger groups, the ILCU appeared to enjoy the full confidence of its affiliates, but feelings about ABCUL were mixed. Many credit unions had other sources of support: local authorities had been increasingly active recently; workplace unions were often supported by their employer; and the Catholic Church played an important role in some British as well as many Irish credit unions.

Most small unions ran weekly collection sessions in church halls or other hired premises, and relied entirely on the services of their own members. The largest unions (in Northern Ireland) had their own offices run by full-time employees. Middle-sized unions – around 800 members – had to decide whether expenditure on staff would be justified in improved administration and higher turnover. Many were reluctant to employ staff for fear that the members would lose control of the union. Some had hired staff without a clear idea about their role, and encountered problems.

Many of the smaller credit unions faced an anxious choice whether to try to expand or to confine their membership. Growth would extend the advantages of membership to more members of the community, and it would provide a firmer financial base. On the other hand, many felt, a large union would destroy the personal approach at the heart of the credit union concept.

### Joining a credit union

The research included personal interviews with a sample of members of seven credit unions. The social composition of the groups varied widely: one consisted mostly of fairly prosperous 'middle class' owner-occupiers; at the other end of the scale, two had recruited mostly unemployed or low-paid council tenants in 'working class' communities. A large proportion of the members of some unions, especially of the two poorest, were women.

Recruitment to credit unions was overwhelmingly by word of mouth, rather than through more formal methods of communication. While better off members had generally been attracted by the prospect of credit at low interest rates, poorer people were more interested in the opportunity to build up their savings. Many members did not really understand what a credit union was when they joined, and it often took them some time to understand how the link between savings and loans worked.

About 10 per cent of members formed a leadership group which was heavily involved in all aspects of the union's activities. Outside this group, only a quarter of the rank and file members had ever attended their union's AGM. Participation (as measured by attendance at meetings) varied strongly from union to union, and was weaker among working class than among middle class members. But there was only one union where non-participation appeared to have induced any feeling of alienation or dissatisfaction. Leaders and participators placed more emphasis on the social and community ideals of the credit union than non-participators did; but it was the poorer, more working class unions which showed most signs of this 'community spirit'.

## Savings

People's ability to budget on their weekly or monthly income was, of course, strongly influenced by how much income they had to budget with. But there were no signs that poor credit union members found the problem either easier or more difficult than other people with similar resources.

More than half of credit union members had savings in building societies, bank deposit accounts and so on. The extent of these savings was largely determined by the family's level of income. The main advantages of the credit union over a building society were said to be convenience and the opportunity to borrow at low rates of interest; the main disadvantage was the low return on the investment.

About two-thirds of members were making regular contributions into their savings account with the credit union. The amount of these regular payments, ranging from 80p to £12.30 per member per week, was largely determined by the union's policy. The longer someone had been a member, the more savings they would have accumulated. Within each union, better-off members tended to build up their savings at a faster rate than those with lower incomes, and this meant that the better-off held a relatively large proportion of the savings pool. High-income families reported even more savings outside the credit union, however, while low income families had placed more than half of their capital with the union.

## Members' use of credit

Although they expressed a clear general preference for credit union loans, the majority of members had used other sources of credit over the past year. The pattern of non-union credit use was similar to that observed in the general population, with better-off families tending to use credit cards, bank loans and store accounts, while poorer people tended to buy on instalments from mail order catalogues. There was no sign that belonging to a credit union reduced people's borrowings from other sources – if anything, the reverse.

Credit union loans were nevertheless used more often than any other single source of credit; three-quarters of all members had had one, just over half within the past year. These loans tended to be between £100 and £500 – that is smaller than bank loans or hire purchase agreements, but larger than most credit transactions with mail order houses or retail outlets. They were used for a wide variety of purposes, led by travel and holidays, vehicles, social celebrations and paying off existing bills. Members reported few problems over the procedures for arranging a loan. Advances tended to be repaid over about a year. The repayment instalments were largely determined by the size of the loan; for a loan of a given size, the instalments were only slightly linked to 'ability to pay' as measured by family income. People with high incomes, however, tended to have borrowed larger sums than those on low incomes. Since the use of non-union credit was also linked with income, it could be seen that the union supplied about two fifths of the credit used by people at all income levels.

## Problems of repayments

A small number of members – most of them poor people – said that they had had some difficulty in repaying money they had borrowed from the credit union. Whether they had experienced problems or not, members thought the debt collection procedures were (or would be) 'sympathetic'. Although it is difficult to use the annual accounts to measure the extent of bad debts, most unions had problem loans, which caused serious difficulties in some cases. Many officers felt that their policies on the allocation of loans and on the recovery of arrears had not been rigorous enough at first, and this had often led to continuing difficulties with debt recovery.

## The value of credit unions

What do these research findings lead to? Are credit unions a good thing or a bad thing? Should they be encouraged, and, if so, how?

Tens of thousands of people belong to credit unions. Few of them are dissatisfied with the way their union is run, feel that there are disadvantages to membership, or wish to leave. If the members want to belong, that is sufficient reason for having a credit union.

Some of the advantages of membership are social and political rather than economic. Although a union depends on the existence of a common bond, it can help to reinforce that bond. The collection meetings are valued as social occasions. Many members may find that the credit union is the only organisation they know which genuinely welcomes equal participation in decision making. Many of those who accept office derive personal satisfaction from their role. For a few, the opportunity to serve and lead their credit union has provided a major step in their personal development.

As in most self-help groups, however, only a small proportion of the members do most of the work, and it is difficult to persuade others to join the leadership group. If people are reluctant to take on these roles, or eager to relinquish them, that is a disadvantage. It also appeared from the survey that rank and file members set much less store by the participative and community spirit ideals than the leaders did. These considerations imply that the social and political advantages of credit unions may not be all that they are cracked up to be by the movement's spokesmen. There is no doubt, though, that they have the edge over impersonal financial institutions on this score.

Many members – a clear majority in some unions – are attracted principally by the opportunity to save. About half of all members hold savings in banks, building societies and so on, but the half who do not are particularly likely to make regular payments into their account with the union. One of the advantages is the convenience of local collection sections, and for those without a previous regular savings plan, the union would be a boon.

There is little sign that credit union members lack access to the mainstream credit market, or that the union substitutes for other kinds of credit. The union is nevertheless members' preferred method of borrowing. This is a clear advantage.

Most credit unions charge an annual percentage rate of interest of 12.7 per cent. This is cheaper than any other source. The banks and building societies charge around 20 per cent, depending on the prevailing rate of interest in the general economy. Other respectable sources charge up to 30 per cent, and charges in the shadier end of the market are much higher than that.

The comparison between credit unions and their nearest rivals is, however, more complicated than declared rates of interest would indicate. Savings have to be taken into account too. A building society offers about 6.5 per cent tax-paid to regular small savers; a bank pays 4 per cent net. The most common credit union dividend is about 4.5 per cent, and many unions, especially the small ones in Great Britain, cannot offer any dividend at all. Secondly, a credit union expects members to leave their savings intact, and take out a loan, if they wish to spend any money. Members are therefore charged for the use of their own money. We asked one of the credit union umbrella organisations, a leading high street bank and a leading building society, each to calculate what would happen to someone with £250

**Table 7.1    Comparison of credit union, bank and building society interest rates**

|  | Credit union | Bank | Building society |
|---|---|---|---|
| **Loan** | | | |
| Amount drawn | £500 | £250[1] | £250[1] |
| Insurance premium | nil[2] | £10.00 | £14.31 |
| Interest rate (apr) | 12.7% | 20.0% | 22.6% |
| Interest charged | £30.40 | £26.67 | £30.41 |
| Repayments (monthly) | £44.20 | £23.89 | £24.56 |
| **Savings** | | | |
| Starting balance | £250 | £250 | £250 |
| Amount withdrawn | nil | £250 | £250 |
| Monthly payments | £42.47 | £62.77 | £62.11 |
| Dividend/interest rate | 4.4%[3] | 4.0%[4] | 6.6%[4] |
| Dividend interest received | £21.28 | £15.06 | £26.31 |
| **Final balance**[5] | £780.92 | £768.30 | £771.63 |

Notes:   1. In practice neither the bank nor the building society would usually offer a personal loan for as small a sum as £250.
2. Most credit unions provide free insurance; banks and building societies add an option premium.
3. The credit union's dividend rate is the average reported in Northern Ireland. Many credit unions, especially in Great Britain, have not been able to offer any dividend.
4. The bank's and building society's interest on savings are after paying composite rate tax. Credit union members would be liable to tax on their dividend if they were tax-payers.
5. If the bank and building society customers did not pay the optional insurance premium, their final balances would be £779.68 and £788.15 respectively.

in savings who wanted to raise £500, and who had £20 per week with which to repay the loan and build up savings over a year. Table 7.1 assumes that the credit union would retain the £250 savings and lend the whole £500; the bank and the building society would release the £250 savings, and lend only £250. At the end of the year, and payments totalling £1290, the credit union member would be only about £10 better off than the member of the building society, or the bank's customer. In fact this advantage depends entirely on assumptions about the provision of insurance, and about the ability of the credit union to pay a dividend. All three creditors agreed that the comparison was not exact, but it is arguable that credit union loans are not much cheaper than credit available from some other sources.

This comparison suggests that there is not much difference between credit unions and other sources of credit, once savings have been taken into account. For people denied access to mainstream credit, the comparison would be much more in the unions' favour. But most credit union members are not in that position.

For the average member, therefore, the credit union provides some social and political benefits; is a convenient method of building up savings; and is the preferred source of credit. These three advantages add up to the conclusion that credit unions are valuable institutions, worthy of encouragement. But as far as the average person is concerned, none of the advantages seems great enough to justify the view that credit unions are superior to all alternatives.

The ideals of the credit union movement are not expressed in terms of the average person, though. Credit unions are aimed principally at poor people, to encourage thrift, and to provide them with a source of cheap credit which will protect them from the clutches of money lenders. It is therefore important to assess unions' impact on families with low incomes.

One of the seven unions studied in detail consisted mainly of middle-income owner-occupiers. It provided a welcome service to those people, but it is fair to conclude that it did little for the poor. The workplace based union included some low paid employees, but few of the poorest people, most of whom have no work at all. Chart 3.2 showed that at least a quarter of the other five unions had incomes near the supplementary benefit (income support) level; in two of them, the proportion of 'poor' members was well over one-third. It is useful to think of poor people as belonging to one of two different types of union: those where they share the union with other people with modest but reasonable incomes; and those where most of their fellow members are about as poor as they are.

None of the credit union members interviewed had borrowed from a money lender within the past year. But several of the poorest among them had made use of trading checks, which are often thought of as 'fringe' credit. It is difficult to draw any conclusions about the effect of credit unions on the use of money lenders, because so little is known about that sector of the market. The survey of 2,155 people recently commissioned by the Office of Fair Trading[1] showed that only one of them used loans from 'a money lender or tallyman' nowadays; two used pawnbrokers; 14 bought on instalments from 'a doorstep salesman or tallyman'. These sources of credit are so rare that the fact that none of the credit union members used them does not necessarily mean very much. Anecdotal evidence suggests that moneylenders are a plague to the poor in certain areas, but it is difficult to say how far credit unions had saved people from their clutches. A recent report suggests that moneylenders are an important cause of debt in the Irish Republic, in spite of the wide availability of credit unions there.[2]

Although we cannot conclude anything about money lenders specifically, it appears that credit unions do not generally replace other forms of credit. The comparison with the OFT survey is not exact, but it shows, if anything, that credit union members are more likely than other people to use other sources of credit such as banks, store cards and hire purchase.

Comparison of the credit union activities of poor and not-so-poor members shows that better-off people save more than poorer ones. This is hardly surprising. It means, first, that unions with a large proportion of poor members take a long time to build up their assets. Second, where there is a range of incomes within a single union, it is the better off who contribute most to the savings pool.

Similarly, better-off members borrow more from their credit union than poorer people do – not more often, but in larger amounts. This is partly because the right to borrow is linked to the member's level of savings; partly because of a higher demand for credit among people who can afford to repay it.

The left hand side of Chart 7.2 summarises the relationship between income and members' savings and loans with the credit union. Both activities are related to income, and it is clear that the

**Chart 7.2    Savings and borrowings of credit union members, by available family income**

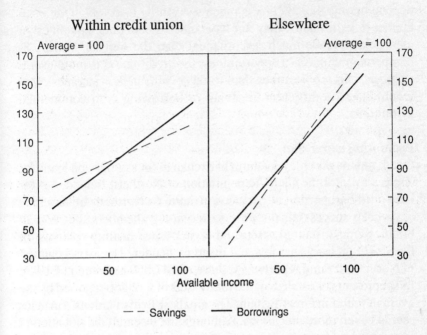

Within credit union          Elsewhere

union is more valuable to people with money than to those without. This may be a disappointment to those whose credit union ideals focus closely on the poor.

Because loans are more strongly related to income than savings are, there is a slight tendency for better-off people to borrow the worse-off members' savings. Better-off people were attracted to join the union by the opportunity to borrow, whereas worse-off people wanted the chance to save. So the relative balance between savings and loans is in accordance with members' own preferences.

The right hand side of Chart 7.2 provides a similar summary of credit union members' activities in the open market – savings with buildings societies, banks and so on; credit from banks, credit cards, mail order and so on. Both savings and borrowings are strongly linked to income. This time, there is a tendency for relatively poor people to borrow the savings of relatively rich people – and to pay them for this service.

But the main point of the chart lies in the comparison between the left hand and right hand sides. Although credit union activities do depend on income, the link is much less strong than it is in the open market. Credit unions may not have created economic equality, but they appear to be much less unequal than the outside world. In comparison with other opportunities, the credit union is more useful to those with low incomes than to those with higher incomes, who would have no difficulty in saving or borrowing with commercial institutions.

## Promoting expansion

Credit unions provide a medium of exchange for savings and loans for about a third of the Catholic population of Northern Ireland, but for only a tiny proportion of people in Britain. In Northern Ireland they have been successful, not only in recruiting members, but also in building up substantial assets and laying down healthy reserves. In Great Britain assets are low and reserves slender. The average union in Northern Ireland reported a reserve of £47,850 at the end of 1986; this represents two-thirds of the total assets of £72,260 reported by the average union in Great Britain. The smallest British unions' finances seemed even more precarious. Although the research did not attempt to establish indicators of financial risk, it may not be surprising that seven of the British unions reviewed in 1987 closed their books during 1988.

It is less than ten years since the British Credit Union Act was passed. Perhaps it is still too early to conclude that the movement has failed to take hold in Britain. But it is clear that credit unions were much better established in Northern Ireland by 1976 than they are in Britain today, and this does not suggest that a long lead-in time is necessary. After a pause in growth between 1982 and 1986, there has been a recent spurt in the establishment of new groups in Britain. It is to be hoped that this is the breakout from an established bridgehead; alternatively, it may be feared that sudden expansion on an uncertain base might overstretch the movement. The newest unions were not included in our research, and it is too early to draw any conclusions about their impact.

An underlying theme for this research has been the conflict between what were called the *idealistic* and *instrumental* approaches to the development of credit unions. It was not intended to imply that this involved an argument between two sets of people who were either wholehearted idealists or pure instrumentalists. Everyone recognises the importance of both considerations; the debate is about where the balance should lie.

There have nevertheless been some fierce, even bitter arguments. One arch instrumentalist claimed that 'credit unions should be a business activity, not a religious experience' – a remark repudiated by his more moderate colleagues. It might be argued that one of the reasons for the slow development of credit unions in Britain has been the polarisation of their supporters: between those whose belief in self-help for the poor has obscured an assessment of the economic realities of the world in which poverty has been created; and those whose narrow focus on the accounts has ignored the social goals which distinguish credit unions from other and stronger financial institutions.

During the early 1980s, the pendulum swung towards the *instrumental* approach. Over the past two or three years the *idealistic* approach has regained ground, but it is important to prevent the pendulum swinging too far the other way. Progress towards the social and anti-poverty goals of credit unions has to based on a hard-headed assessment of the economic and financial constraints within which they operate.

One of the focal points for the debate within the movement is the question of scale. *Instrumental* considerations favour credit unions with thousands of members and substantial assets. In North America mergers have created credit unions big enough to compete on level terms with many commercial finance houses. There is talk of this happening on a smaller scale in Northern Ireland. *Idealistic* considerations favour small credit unions where everyone knows everyone else, and actively participates in running the scheme. But the research suggests that a sense of participation is not as important to the rank and file members as their leaders think; moreover there is no clear evidence that the feeling of belonging varies between credit unions of different size.

It might be argued that any advantages to be gained by restricting membership to two or three hundred people would be outweighed by the financial risk of operating on so small a base. Yet three-quarters of all British unions have fewer than 300 members. Once a union had achieved financial stability, on the other hand, there would be no point in recruiting additional members to the point at which the common bond could be diluted or forgotten. The ideal size for any particular union will depend on the priorities of its existing members, and on the number of people within the scope of the common bond. In general, it might be suggested, unions should aim for about 500 members in the first instance – about as many as can be administered by volunteers without straining their goodwill. Those groups still with plenty of demand at that stage might then aim to grow again, to stabilise with a membership of about 1,500 serviced by a paid administrator.

Very large institutions such as the big American credit unions or British building societies depend primarily on their performance in the open market for savings and credit. But groups with a few hundred or even a few thousand members depend heavily on loyalty to the common bond to persuade people to save regularly, repay their loans and contribute time and energy to administration. It is therefore important to assess the research evidence about common bonds.

The strength of credit unions among Catholics in Northern Ireland might be explained by a sense of common cause within a minority group which felt oppressed by the majority. But this theory scarcely explains the high level of credit union membership in the Republic of Ireland. A more plausible explanation for unions' performance North and South of the border lies in the connection with the Catholic church. Even though unions in Ireland usually define their potential membership in terms of a geographical area, the actual common bond probably lies in membership of the church. Apart from any material advantages to be gained through the use of church halls and so on, active support from the pulpit and the existing hierarchy and discipline especially associated with the Catholic church provide an ideal environment for a credit union.

This link cannot be expected to be as useful in Britain. Catholics form a minority of the population, and (outside the enclaves of Irish immigration in Glasgow, Lancashire and London) they are dispersed among the non-Catholic population. Even so, three of the four (non-workplace) British unions included in our survey served a largely Catholic membership. Other churches might take on a similar role, though the less formal relationship between ministers and parishioners might limit the number of people who would consider themselves committed to the common bond. While a credit union might usefully be established among existing members of a church, there is no sign that unions with Christian origins have been particularly successful in attracting members from the community at large.

Another existing structure on which credit unions can be based is the workplace. All the potential members have regular incomes, and it is easy to deduct regular savings or repayment instalments direct from pay. Employers are usually willing to provide some form of support. These administrative arrangements are so satisfactory that a credit union can operate successfully with relatively little commitment of time or enthusiasm by its members. The workplace credit union included in our survey seemed to have the lowest morale, and had been in danger of collapse through lack of interest; it had nevertheless managed to build up savings more rapidly than any of the other unions under study. There are, however, two drawbacks. One is that the union may add to members' sense of dependency on their employer, rather than encourage independence through self-help. The second is that the union automatically excludes people without jobs, who may be the poorest and in greatest need of its services.

The *idealistic* aims of credit unions therefore depend heavily on the 'community' common bond. All the signs are, though, that this is the most difficult base on which to build. The people of some areas may have a natural bond: perhaps because of a clear boundary between one housing estate and another; perhaps because of a concentration of members of one ethnic group; perhaps because at some stage the people made common cause against the municipal bureaucracy; perhaps through working for a single employer; perhaps through support of a successful football team. Where such a bond exists, a credit union might thrive, and could help to cement the original relationship.

In areas where none of these things have generated a sense of community, a credit union will face more serious difficulties. Poverty may provide a common bond when everyone can identify the same external cause (like the pit owners, for example), but most 'poor' areas contain a mixture of well paid and under paid employees, successful and unsuccessful people who have set up on their own, unemployed, sick and retired people. Many poor families feel ashamed of themselves or 'different' from their neighbours. In those circumstances, poverty can be a divisive rather than a cohesive force. A credit union could establish itself only by creating a common bond from scratch – a sense of loyalty to the union itself.

There are enough examples of credit unions operating within ordinary communities to show that this can be done, given talented leadership and local good will. Not surprisingly, they find it an uphill struggle. The question is: how can they be encouraged and supported?

One possibility might be to combine the advantages of different types of bond by opening a credit union to the employees of a firm *and* the residents of the surrounding area. This might be a particularly powerful combination either if local authorities wished to promote credit unions, or in towns with a single dominant employer.

There are four ways in which outsiders might help a community credit union to start up.

*Stimulus*: Obviously, the first step is to let people know that credit unions exist, and what they can achieve. This can be done in general by giving lectures and film shows, encouraging stories in local papers and radio programmes, distributing leaflets and so on. We were told that there was no point in 'selling' credit unions – calling a meeting on a housing estate specifically to suggest one – and that the initiative should come from the potential members. But some of the development workers hired to promote credit unions within local authority areas may come close to 'selling'.

*Expertise*: The description of running a credit union in Chapter 2 made it clear that the leaders required a substantial contribution of advice and training at the start. Some of this has to be explicit instruction; on other issues, leaders need to be told what choices are open to them, and left to take their own decisions. It is not clear whether outside supporters should also actively help the leadership team during the formative period, as well as instructing and advising them.

*Expenditure subsidy*: Some unions have managed to obtain small one-off grants to meet or contribute to start-up costs associated with registration and recruitment. Others have received more substantial funds to pay for staff or other running costs over the first two or three years. These initial subsidies have not always been successful. It might be argued that they had not been thought out properly beforehand. A more general objection might lie in the difficulty of 'weaning' a group off its subsidy after the initial period.

*Capital subsidy*: An external supporter might subsidise the assets of a new credit union. There have been one or two cases of a credit union being launched with a benefactor's contribution to the capital fund. The Credit Union Act forbids such subsidies being offered as a loan.

If more community credit unions are to be set up, there is no doubt that the supporters of the movement will have to spread the word about the advantages of membership, and provide information, advice and training to the leaders of embryo groups. There are serious doubts whether assistance should go any further than that. In the long run, a community credit union depends on the loyalty of its members, and on the willingness of some of them to work for the common good. It is feared that too much support might allow unions to develop among groups of people lacking the necessary commitment; worse, that if life is too easy at the start, the commitment will actually be discouraged. This is the Spartan philosophy. Experience shows that idealistic outsiders cannot create credit unions in areas of need. But it is worth looking for ways of delivering support which encourage success without damping down commitment.

This research has focussed on the credit unions themselves, rather than on the various organisations which support and control them. In Ireland there is one organisation which promotes and supports credit unions, and takes a large share of the responsibility for supervising them. The Irish League appears to be a strong and effective organisation based on the resources provided indirectly by 750,000 individual members.

In Britain, there is no single organisation responsible for the development of credit unions. The Association of British Credit Unions has been the larger of the two umbrella groups. In the past it has been over-committed to an *instrumental* view of credit union development, and has faced administrative and financial problems. More recently, however, the Association has broadened its policy, and a change of personnel and location is said to have led to improved administration. The National Federation of Credit Unions stood out for the *idealistic* approach. For many years it had only ten member unions, but it has been responsible for a large share of the growth in numbers that has been achieved in the past year or so.

There are still only 35,000 credit union members in Great Britain. They cannot afford the luxury of two national associations. The differences between the two groups may seem important to the protagonists, but there is no reason why a policy could not be worked out within a 'broad church'. To outsiders the split has all the appearance of a sectarian squabble.

Another institution involved with credit unions is the Registry of Friendly Societies. It has fulfilled its statutory duties, and reports that no member has ever lost money through the failure of a union. But there have been various indications in the course of our research project that this very minor aspect of the Registry's work has been channeled into a bureaucratic backwater. That would not matter if (as in Ireland) some other organisation effectively held the reins, but lack of interest within the Registry may have contributed to the weakness of the movement in Britain.

Another group of potential supporters is local authorities. Several have hired credit union development workers, or have supported workers employed by one of the umbrella organisations. Many have been appointed quite recently, and more posts have been announced. It has not yet been possible to assess their work. They will provide a welcome addition to credit unions' resources within the cities and counties where they have been appointed. On the other hand, our research identified a number of initiatives of this sort which had not been thought through in advance, and which were not successful. In other cases, the ambitions of the local authority did not accord with the experience of the umbrella organisations. Care is needed to harness the resources provided by local authorities to promote the best strategy for unions and their members.

While the existing credit unions provide a valuable service to a growing number of people, there is some doubt whether they can ever 'take off' to reach a substantial proportion of the population in Great Britain, in the absence of a widespread natural common bond equivalent to the Catholic church in Ireland, and in competition with existing and widely available sources of credit. If there is to be any chance at all, it may be suggested, there should be a single agency responsible for the encouragement, support and regulation of all unions. This might take one of two forms.

One of the options lies within the direct control of the existing credit unions. It would be achieved if the existing umbrella groups joined to form a single union of credit unions. This would have no chance of success if members, officers or staff of either existing organisation entered the merger anxious to achieve as much as possible for their own side. It could work if both sides recognised that they had failed in the past and contributed to an entirely new body. The organisation would combine the services provided to credit unions by the two existing groups, and develop a coherent but wide-ranging development strategy. It would put this into effect in collaboration with the Registry of Friendly Societies, local authorities or any other available ally.

This option would retain the self-determination which many credit union members value. But it would remain a small and relatively weak body, dependent on individual negotiations with others for support. An alternative form of organisation would be based on a formal alliance between the unions themselves, on the one hand, and representatives of other interest groups, on the other. These could include public agencies such as the Registrar of Friendly Societies, the Office of Fair Trading and the National Consumer Council; local authority interests; the churches; other voluntary organisations; and charities wishing to support the movement. Such an agency would probably have some official status as a quango. The Registry of Friendly Societies might outpost its registration staff to work with the new organisation, in order to maximise the liaison between development and policing activities. It would probably attract a small endowment of public money, at least to cover its secretariat and enforcement costs. It would provide insurance and banking facilities to the member unions, and this would raise revenue with which to pay for other services. It would look for grant aid from central or local government, or from charities, to pay for development work.

It is assumed that any new Credit Union Development Agency would cover Great Britain. There is no need for any change in Northern Ireland, and it would be pointless to break up the successful Irish League. It is to be hoped that Protestant credit unions in Northern Ireland would join the League. But they might be allowed to join and register with the British agency if their members refused any association with Dublin.

The proposal for a single agency puts all the credit union eggs in one basket. If the system of political patronage led to the appointment of a weak Chair; if the credit unions and the other members could not reach an agreed policy; if the unions indulged in factional strife among themselves; or if the other interests were less than wholehearted in their support – if any of these things happened, the agency could fail, and with it the hopes of the credit union movement. Such an agency may nevertheless represent the best chance for credit unions in the 1990s.

## References
1. Public Attitude Surveys Ltd, *Consumer Credit Survey*, 1988.
2. M. Daly and J. Walsh, *Money Lending and Low Income Families*, Combat Poverty Agency, Dublin, 1988.

# Appendix: The Survey of Members

## Sample
The survey covered the members of seven credit unions. An eighth was approached, but its officers preferred not to take part. We decided not to take a systematic random sample of all credit unions in the United Kingdom. We were, for example, more interested in the difficulties experienced in Great Britain than in the more successful credit unions in Northern Ireland, but a systematic random sample would have provided six times as many interviews in Ulster as in Britain. The selection was designed as far as possible to cover each type of union (community, association and workplace), in different parts of the United Kingdom. The group included large and medium-sized unions, but not very small ones.

The officers of each of the seven unions agreed to go through their records to identify every nth member, using a procedure designed to yield 25 members who currently had a loan outstanding, and 25 without a current loan. The union wrote to each of the selected members, telling them about the survey, and giving them an opportunity to refuse to release their name and address. Details of those who had not opted out were passed to PSI to take part in the survey.

Each of the credit unions' members were interviewed by a different interviewer. All the interviewers had experience of work of this kind. Five were briefed in person; the sixth by telephone. The briefings were backed up by detailed written instructions.

A copy of the questionnaire is attached at the end of this appendix.

Interviews took place in members' homes, not at the credit union's premises. The interview was with the named member as selected by the union. If that person was married, information was collected about the couple's income, savings and non-union credit use. If the spouse was also a union member (independently of the named respondent) details of his or her union savings and loans were also obtained. Interviewers were instructed to involve the spouse in the interview whenever possible, especially if the spouse was the person mainly responsible for the family's money management.

The response among members of each of the seven unions was as follows:

| | |
|---|---|
| Suburb | 38 interviews |
| Borough | 22 interviews |
| Yorkshire | 36 interviews |
| Belfast | 30 interviews |
| N. Ireland | 32 interviews |
| Northern | 34 interviews |
| Scotland | 39 interviews |

The low response rate in the Borough credit union appeared to be associated with its status as a workplace based credit union. Members associated the union with their work, and were reluctant to give up their leisure time to be interviewed about it.

The completed interview schedules were checked and coded in the office, and subject to a computer edit check before analysis. Those questionnaires with a 'don't know' at certain key questions were analysed in comparison with the others in order to calculate an estimate of the correct answer. For example, earnings were estimated on the basis of occupation, savings on the basis of their known relationship with income.

At the analysis stage, the results were reweighted to provide a) equal representation from each of the seven unions, and b) the correct proportion of people with and without loans among the membership of each union.

The sample as selected was representative of all members. This is the appropriate basis for analysis of procedures associated with membership such as participation in union activities, savings and loans. Where the analysis covers 'outside' factors such as income and employment, non-union savings and the use of non-union credit, it is more appropriate to look at member-families as a unit. The same approach is needed for a comparison between within-union and outside activities (such as total savings). Where both members of a couple were members of the union, it was necessary to apply a half weight in order to make the sample representative of member families. Each table carries a note (at the top right) to show whether it is representative of members or of member-families. The non-technical reader need not bother with this distinction.

Within the usual limits (of sampling error, response bias and measurement accuracy) the results of the survey provide an accurate representation of each of the seven unions. As mentioned in the introduction, however, the combined results for all seven unions cannot be considered truly representative of all unions in the UK. First, the seven were not a random selection, and clearly differ in some respects from a true cross-section. Second, the variation between unions (especially in their social composition, and in their savings policies) were so great that there can be little statistical confidence in the findings based on only seven. Third, the decision to assign equal weight to each union (rather than a weight proportionate to its membership) means that the sample will be more representative of unions than of union members.

When there are big differences between unions, therefore, it is not strictly correct to add them together. In practice we have sometimes added them, but this should be read only as an approximation, and we have also indicated the range of variation between them. Where the unions all provide similar results, there is no reason not to combine them, and we can be much more confident that this accurately reflects the national picture.

It is for this reason that it has been necessary to describe differences between unions in more detail than might have seemed appropriate in a report which was more concerned with the overall state of credit unions than with the condition of particular groups.

## Survey about Credit Unions

| | Col/ code | Go to |
|---|---|---|
| | | 103 |

Interviewer _____     Union/Interview number [    ][ ]     101 → 103

| | 104 |
|---|---|

Date of interview _____     Time started _____ Card  ①  → 104

---

1a. I'm working on a survey of members of the _____ Credit Union. It's part of a survey all over the country, to find out what people think about credit unions, and how the services work.

I've got down the name of _____ (NAMED RESPONDENT) as the member of the _____ Credit Union who I should talk to. Can I just check before we start, are you now married or single?

| | 105 | |
|---|---|---|
| Married | 1 | |
| Single (or ex-married) | 2 | Q2 |

IF NOW SINGLE, TURN PAGE TO Q2
IF MARRIED, CONTINUE
b) Is your husband/wife also a member of the credit union, with a separate account, or is there just the one membership?

| | 106 |
|---|---|
| Spouse is separate member | 1 |
| Only one membership | 2 |

NOTE: ALL QUESTIONS REFER TO MEMBERSHIP BY NAMED
RESPONDENT, UNLESS SPECIFIC REFERENCE TO SPOUSE

CONTINUE WITH ALL MARRIED
c) Which of the two of you usually deals with shopping and money matters, or do both of you get involved?

| | 107 | |
|---|---|---|
| Named respondent deals with shopping/money | 1 | A |
| Spouse deals with with shopping/money | 2 | B |
| Both get involved | 3 | C |

FOLLOW INSTRUCTION A, B OR C:

A: (NAMED RESP. DEALS) Interview named respondent

B: (SPOUSE DEALS) Interview named respondent and spouse together

C: (BOTH INVOLVED) Interview named respondent, with or without spouse

CODE TYPE OF INTERVIEW

| | 108 |
|---|---|
| Joint interview | 1 |
| Named respondent above | 2 |

- 1 -

## Joining the Credit Union

**2a.** When did you join the credit union?

`109,10`

Year **1 9**

**b.** How did you find out about the credit union? READ OUT BOLD HEADINGS, AND PROBE TO CODE

| | |
|---|---|
| **Did someone from the credit union get in touch with you:** | `111` |
| ... come to see you | 1 |
| or ring you on the telephone | 2 |
| or did they send you a leaflet | 3 |
| **Or did you hear about it some other way:** | |
| ... by seeing an advertisement | 4 |
| or by talking to friends or relatives | 5 |
| (Was involved in union from start; finding out about it not relevant) | 6 |

**c.** When you first heard about credit unions, were you keen on the idea straight away, or were you a bit doubtful to start with?

`112`

| | | |
|---|---|---|
| Keen straight away | 1 | f |
| Doubtful to start with | 2 | |

IF DOUBTFUL TO START WITH
d) Why do you say that?
RECORD IN FULL

`113`

e) Did anything in particular make you change your mind?
RECORD IN FULL

`114`

ALL
**f.** When you joined the credit union, what was your reason?
RECORD IN FULL

`115`

SHOW CARD A
**g.** Which of these reasons comes closest to explaining why you joined?

`116`

| | |
|---|---|
| because you thought it would be helpful to you personally? | 1 |
| or because you thought a credit union would be helpful to other people? | 2 |
| or because you thought having a credit union would get people together and create a community spirit? | 3 |
| or did you join mainly because you were asked to do so? | 4 |

**h.** When you joined did you expect ..... READ OUT

`117`

| | |
|---|---|
| that it would be a useful way for you to save | 1 |
| or that it would be a useful way for you to borrow | 2 |
| or were you not interested in saving or borrowing? | 3 |

IF BOTH PROBE
Which was more important to you at the time?

- 2 -

# Involvement in Union Activities

**3a** Were you one of the people who was involved in getting the credit union going?

|  |  | 118 |
|---|---|---|
|  | Yes | 1 |
|  | No | 2 |

**b.** Are you one of the directors of the credit union at the moment, or are you on any committee, or are you just a member?
RECORD DETAILS OF CURRENT ROLES, THEN PROBE TO CODE

**c.** Have you ever had any (other) position in the credit union since you joined?
RECORD DETAILS OF PREVIOUS ROLES, THEN PROBE TO CODE

Current _____

_____

_____ Board of directors/main committee:

|  |  | Present 119 | Previous 120 |  |
|---|---|---|---|---|
| _____ | with title | 1 | 1 | |
| Previous _____ | no title | 2 | 2 | |
| Other committee(s): | with title | 3 | 3 | |
| _____ | no title | 4 | 4 | |
| _____ No committee(s) | | 5 | 5 | e |

IF NOW/PREVIOUSLY A DIRECTOR/COMMITTEE MEMBER (ANY CODE 1 - 4)
**d)** How long have you been (were you) a director/committee member for? PROBE FOR TOTAL YEARS SERVICE

|  |  | 121,22 |
|---|---|---|
|  | Years | |

IF NOW A DIRECTOR/COMMITTEE MEMBER, SKIP TO g
IF NOT NOW A DIRECTOR/COMMITTEE MEMBER ('Present' CODE 5)
**e)** Do you do anything to help the credit union at the moment - as a collector or organiser or something?

|  |  | 123 |  |
|---|---|---|---|
|  | Yes (_____) EXPLAIN | 1 | g |
|  | No | 2 | |

IF NO
**f)** Would you be interested in spending any time helping to run the credit union, or are you happy just to be an ordinary member?

|  |  | 124 |  |
|---|---|---|---|
|  | Interested in helping | 1 | Q4 |
|  | Happy as ordinary member | 2 | Q4 |

IF NOW DIRECTOR/COMMITTEE MEMBER/HELPER
**g)** Would you like to spend more of your time helping to run the credit union; or do you feel you spend too much time on it and want to cut down?

|  |  | 125 |
|---|---|---|
|  | Like to spend more time | 1 |
|  | Spends too much time | 2 |
|  | Neither - happy with present arrangement | 3 |

- 3 -

| | | AGM | Education sessions | Social gather | Other meetings |
|---|---|---|---|---|---|
| | | 126 | 127 | 128 | 129 |
| | Regularly attended | 1 | 1 | 1 | 1 |
| | Sometimes | 2 | 2 | 2 | 2 |
| | Rarely/just once | 3 | 3 | 3 | 3 |
| | Never attended | 4 | 4 | 4 | 4 |

**4a.** Have you ever attended the Annual General Meeting of the credit union? IF YES Have you attended regularly, sometimes, or just once? CODE IN GRID BELOW

**b.** Have you been to any 'education sessions' when they tell you how the credit union works, and teach you how to handle money and credit and so on?

**c.** Have you been to any social gatherings organised for members?

**d.** Have you attended other meetings for members?

f
f
f

IF NEVER ATTENDED ANY (ALL CODE 4s)
e) Is there any particular reason why you haven't been to any meetings? RECORD IN FULL

130

8

IF EVER ATTENDED ANY
f) Have you been going to credit union meetings <u>more often</u> recently, compared with when you first joined, or <u>less often</u>; or has your attendance stayed about the same?

131

| | |
|---|---|
| More often recently | 1 |
| Less often | 2 |
| The same | 3 |

ALL
**g.** Do you think you've got to know more people as a result of joining the credit union? PROBE TO CODE

132

| | |
|---|---|
| Yes, lots of people | 1 |
| Yes, some people | 2 |
| No | 3 |

**h.** Has the credit union helped to give you personally a feeling of 'belonging'?

133

| | |
|---|---|
| Yes, definitely | 1 |
| Yes, slightly | 2 |
| No | 3 |

**i.** Do you think the credit union has given its members generally a feeling of belonging, and created a community spirit?

134

| | |
|---|---|
| Yes, definitely | 1 |
| Yes, slightly | 2 |
| No, not really | 3 |
| No, definitely not | 4 |

- 4 -

ALL RESPONDENTS

5a. How satisfied are you with the way the credit union is run at the moment. Are you ... READ OUT     135

| | |
|---|---|
| very satisfied | 1 |
| fairly satisfied | 2 | Q6 |
| rather dissatisfied | 3 | Q6 |
| or very dissatisfied? | 4 |

IF VERY SATISFIED OR VERY DISSATISFIED
b) Why do you say that?
RECORD IN FULL     136

---

6a. Who do you think has the most influence over the way the credit union is run: the directors and committees, or the ordinary members?     137

| | |
|---|---|
| Directors/committees | 1 |
| Ordinary members | 2 |

b. Do you think it would be better if _____ (READ OUT EACH IN TURN) had more influence and control over the running of the union; or would you rather they had less influence, or do you think things are alright as they are?

| | Directors Committee members | Ordin- ary members | |
|---|---|---|---|
| | 138 | 139 | |
| Should have more influence and control | 1 | 1 | |
| ... less influence and control | 2 | 2 | |
| Things alright as they are | 3 | 3 | Q7 |

IF ANY CHANGE NEEDED (CODES 1 or 2)
c) Why do you say that? PROBE What are the problems with the present arrangements?
RECORD IN FULL     140

## Circumstances

ALL RESPONDENTS

7   So far we've been talking just about the credit union. In a moment, I'd like to
ask about any savings or loans you may have, not just with the credit union,
but with all kinds of other places as well. Before that, I need to find out
something about your own circumstances.

ASK a TO c ABOUT RESPONDENT; REPEAT FOR SPOUSE IF MARRIED

a   (i) Do you yourself work at the moment, or what do you do?
(ii) Does your husband/wife work at the moment, or what does he/she do?

PROBE TO CODE

| | Resp't 141 | Spouse 142 | |
|---|---|---|---|
| WORKING.....Employed full-time | 1 | 1 | |
| Employed part-time | 2 | 2 | |
| Self-employed | 3 | 3 | |
| NOT WORKING......Seeking work | 4 | 4 | |
| Sick or disabled | 5 | 5 | next |
| Bringing up children | 6 | 6 | next |
| Housewife | 7 | 7 | next |
| Retired | 8 | 8 | next |

IF WORKING OR SEEKING WORK

b) Can you tell me what work you do (he/she does)?
RECORD FULL DETAILS OF PRESENT OR LAST JOB

| Respondent   Spouse | 143,44 | 145,46 |
|---|---|---|
| | | |

IF WORKING

c) How much do you (does he/she) earn in <u>take-home</u> pay? IF VARIES, PROBE How
much was your/his/her last payment?

| | 147,51 | 152,56 |
|---|---|---|
| £ | 157 | 158 |
| per week | 1 | 1 |
| per fortnight | 2 | 2 |
| per month | 4 | 4 |
| per year | 6 | 6 |
| other periods | 8 | 8 |
| (EXPLAIN_____) | | |

NB IF ANNUAL SALARY GIVEN
CHECK IF THIS IS GROSS
OR AFTER TAX ETC. PROBE
FOR NET AMOUNT - MONTHLY?
RECORD GROSS FIGURE
ONLY IF DK NET

SHOW CARD B

8.  Do you (and your husband/wife) receive any benefits from the DHSS or the
    local council, like the ones on this card? GO THROUGH EACH IN TURN                159

                                          Child benefit (or family allowance)          1
                                                        Retirement pension             2
                                                      Unemployment benefit             3
                                                        Disability benefit             4
                                                     Supplementary benefit             5
                                                   Family income supplement            6
                                        Housing benefit (rent/rates rebates)           7
                                                          Any other benefits

                                                  (EXPLAIN_____           8

                                                            _____         9

                                                  No benefits                          0    c

    IF ANY BENEFITS RECEIVED
    b) How much do you receive (for each of these)?                        160,62

        A_____(benefit): £___.___ per _____

                                                                           163,65

        B_____(benefit): £___.___ per _____

                                                                           166,68

        C_____(benefit): £___.___ per _____

                                                                           169,71

        D_____(benefit): £___.___ per _____

c)  Do (either of) you have any other kinds of income that we haven't mentioned?
    Things like ... READ OUT IN TURN                                                   172

                                          A pension from a former employer?            1
                                      A pension from a private insurance plan?          2
                                                      Maintenance payments?             3
                            A second job or business, or occasional earnings?           4
                                                  Income from savings?                  5
                                                          None of these                 6    Q9

    IF ANY OF THESE INCOMES
    d) How much do you receive (for each of these)?                        173,75

        A_____(income): £___.___ per _____

                                                                           176,78

        B_____(income): £___.___ per _____                              (CARD 2)

                                                                           205,07

        C_____(income): £___.___ per _____

- 7 -

| | 9a. | When you're thinking about budgeting, do you tend to count up how much you spend over a _week_, or a _month_; or what period do you use? | | 208 | |
|---|---|---|---|---|---|

9a. When you're thinking about budgeting, do you tend to count up how much you spend over a <u>week</u>, or a <u>month</u>; or what period do you use?

|  |  | 208 |
|---|---|---|
|  | Week | 1 |
| USE BUDGET PERIOD NAMED HERE WHEN ASKING b and c | Fortnight | 2 |
|  | Month | 4 |
|  | Quarter | 5 |
|  | Year | 6 |
|  | Other period | 8 |
|  | (EXPLAIN _____) | |

b. Do you ever manage to put any money away for things like bills, new clothes and so on that don't come up every week/month? PROBE TO CODE BELOW

c. Do you ever run out of money too soon, before your next 'pay day', so you're in trouble to last out the week/month?

| | a Put away 209 | b Run out 210 |
|---|---|---|
| Yes - most weeks/months | 1 | 1 |
| - More often than not | 2 | 2 |
| - Sometimes | 3 | 3 |
| - Hardly ever | 4 | 4 |
| No, never | 5 | 5 |

d. On the whole, would you say you are ...READ OUT

| | 211 |
|---|---|
| Managing quite well on your money | 1 |
| or just getting by | 2 |
| or getting into difficulties? | 3 |

e. Are you behind with any payments, or do you owe any money at present?

| | 212 |
|---|---|
| Yes | 1 |
| No | 2 | Q10

IF YES, COMPLETE GRID, AND PROBE Do you owe for anything else, or are you behind with anything else at present?

| What do you owe for What are you behind with? | Who do you owe for that | OFFICE USE | How much do you owe for that? |
|---|---|---|---|
| (i) | | 213,14 | 215,18 £ |
| (ii) | | 219,20 | 221,24 £ |
| (iii) | | 225,26 | 227,30 £ |
| (iv) | | 231,32 | 233,36 £ |

- 8 -

## Savings with Credit Union

10a | CHECK Q1 WHETHER MARRIED AND WHETHER SPOUSE A MEMBER OF CREDIT UNION. | 237
| | |
| Unmarried | 1
| Married - spouse not a separate member | 2
| - spouse a member - present at interview | 3
| CHOOSE CODE 4 OR 5    - resp't able to give details | 4
| AFTER ASKING Q10b    - resp't not able to give details | 5

b. Now I'd like to ask about any money you (and your husband/wife) are saving with the _____ Credit Union. Do you have a plan to save so much regularly every week or month? PROBE And what about your husband/wife?

|  | Resp't | Spouse |  |
|---|---|---|---|
|  | 238 | 239 |  |
| Yes, regular payments now........... | 1 | 1 |  |
| No regular payments PROBE ... in past | 2 | 2 | Q11 |
| ... never | 3 | 3 | Q11 |
|  | 240,42 | 243,45 |  |

IF REGULAR PAYMENTS NOW
c) How much are your regular payments?                                     £

|  | 246 | 247 |
|---|---|---|
| per week | 1 | 1 |
| per fortnight | 2 | 2 |
| per month | 4 | 4 |
| per quarter | 5 | 5 |
| other periods | 8 | 8 |
| EXPLAIN_____ | | |

SHOW CARD C
d) How is the regular payment made: do you pay over cash, or is it deducted from pay, or what? PROBE TO CODE

|  | 248 | 249 |
|---|---|---|
| Cash/cheque taken to collection point | 1 | 1 |
| Cash/cheque collected from your home | 2 | 2 |
| Cash/cheque sent by post | 3 | 3 |
| Standing order from bank/building society | 4 | 4 |
| Deduction from earnings paid direct to credit union | 5 | 5 |

CARD C AGAIN
d) Do you think that is the best way of making regular payments, or would you prefer a different method? IF PREFER DIFFERENT What would be a better way?

|  | 250 | 251 |
|---|---|---|
| Way used is best | 0 | 0 |
| Prefer different    Cash/cheque taken to collection point | 1 | 1 |
| Cash/cheque collected from your home | 2 | 2 |
| Cash/cheque sent by post | 3 | 3 |
| Standing order from bank/building society | 4 | 4 |
| Deduction from earnings paid direct to credit union | 5 | 5 |

- 9 -

| 11a | (Apart from _regular_ payments,) do you ever manage to make any payments into your savings with the credit union from time to time? | | | |
|---|---|---|---|---|

| | Resp't 252 | Spouse 253 | |
|---|---|---|---|
| Makes payments from time to time | 1 | 1 | |
| No payments | 2 | 2 | Q12 |

IF MAKES PAYMENTS FROM TIME TO TIME
b) How many times have you made a payment into your savings with the credit union in the _past three months_? and how much have you paid, altogether, in that time?

| | 254 | 255 |
|---|---|---|
| Number of payments over three months | | |
| | 256,58 | 259,61 |
| Amount paid in total £ | | |

| 12a | Can you tell me how much you have saved in credit union shares, at the moment? RECORD AMOUNT AND CODE ACCURACY |
|---|---|

| | 262,65 | 266,69 |
|---|---|---|
| £ | | |
| | 270 | 271 |
| Exact amount known | 1 | 1 |
| Approximate amount known | 2 | 2 |
| Amount unknown, but has savings | 3 | 3 |
| No savings – known | 4 | 4 |
| Not known whether savings or not | 5 | 5 |

NOMINAL SHARES (eg £1, £10) REQUIRED FOR MEMBERSHIP CODE 4

c
Q13

IF HAS SAVINGS
b) Are your savings in credit union shares more or less now, compared with this time last year?

| | 272 | 273 | |
|---|---|---|---|
| More | 1 | 1 | Q13 |
| Less | 2 | 2 | Q13 |
| About the same | 3 | 3 | Q13 |

IF NO SAVINGS NOW (CODE 4 at a)
c) Have you ever had any money saved with the credit union in the past?

| | 274 | 275 |
|---|---|---|
| Yes, saved in past | 1 | 1 |
| No, never | 2 | 2 |

d) Is there any particular reason why you do not have any money saved with the credit union at the moment?
RECORD IN FULL

| | 276 | 277 |
|---|---|---|
| | | |

e) Do you expect to save with the credit union in future, or not?

| | 278 | 279 |
|---|---|---|
| Yes, expects to save | 1 | 1 |
| No, does not expect to | 2 | 2 |
| Don't know/not sure | 3 | 3 |

- 10 -

(CARD 3)

ALL RESPONDENTS

13a. Can you tell me what dividend people earn on their savings with the
_____ credit union? RECORD BELOW; IF 'NO DIVIDEND PAID' RECORD ZERO

b. And do you know what interest most people get on their savings with building societies?

|  | Credit union 305,06 | Building societies 307,08 |
|---|---|---|
| Dividend/Interest rate % | | |
| | 309 | 310 |
| per month | 1 | 1 |
| per year | 2 | 2 |
| other periods | 3 | 3 |
| Rate not known | 8 | 8 |

14a. Apart from a savings account, do you (or your husband/wife) belong to any other schemes run by the credit union, such as ... READ OUT EACH IN TURN?

|  | Christmas club | Clothing club | Holiday club | Other scheme |
|---|---|---|---|---|
| NB: CHECK NOT COUNTED AS SAVINGS ABOVE | 311 | 312 | 313 | 314 |
| Respondent a member | 1 | 1 | 1 | 1 |
| Spouse a member | 2 | 2 | 2 | 2 |
| Not a member | 3 | 3 | 3 | 3 |
| FOR EACH MEMBERSHIP b) How much do you have saved at present? £ | 315,17 | 318,20 | 321,23 | 324,26 |
| | | | | |
| c) How much is your regular subscription? £ | 327,29 | 330,32 | 333,35 | 336,38 |
| | | | | |
| | 339 | 340 | 341 | 342 |
| per week | 1 | 1 | 1 | 1 |
| per fortnight | 2 | 2 | 2 | 2 |
| per month | 4 | 4 | 4 | 4 |
| other periods | 8 | 8 | 8 | 8 |
| EXPLAIN_____ | | | | |

Next

- 11 -

## Other Savings

15a Now I'd like to ask about any other savings you may have, apart from the credit union. Do you (or your husband/wife) have any money saved at the moment with ... READ OUT IN TURN? IF NO, PROBE Have you ever had any savings with _____ in the past?

FOR EACH CURRENTLY USED

b) Do you have a plan to save so much regularly every week or every month with _____?

c) How much do you have in your savings account with _____?
   IF MORE THAN ONE ACCOUNT, ADD TOGETHER

d) Is that more or less than you had saved with them this time last year?

| | | A building society | Bank dpst accnt | The Post Office | Any other types | |
|---|---|---|---|---|---|---|
| | | 343 | 344 | 345 | 346 | b |
| a) Savings | Now | 1 | 1 | 1 | 1 | |
| | In past | 2 | 2 | 2 | 2 | next |
| | Never | 3 | 3 | 3 | 3 | next |
| | | 347 | 348 | 349 | 350 | |
| b) Regular payments | Yes | 1 | 1 | 1 | 1 | |
| | No | 2 | 2 | 2 | 2 | |
| | | 351,54 | 355,58 | 359,62 | 363,366 | |
| c) Amount | £ | | | | | |
| | | 367 | 368 | 369 | 370 | |
| d) Compared with last year | More | 1 | 1 | 1 | 1 | |
| | Less | 2 | 2 | 2 | 2 | |
| | About the same | 3 | 3 | 3 | 3 | |

e. Apart from savings, do you have an ordinary current account for handling regular money ... READ OUT IN TURN

(CARD 4

| | 405.07 | |
|---|---|---|
| | Yes | No |
| ... with a bank? | 1 | 2 |
| ... with a building society? | 1 | 2 |
| ... with the post office? | 1 | 2 |

- 12 -

| | | |
|---|---|---|
| 16a | What would you say are the <u>advantages</u> for people who save with the credit union, compared with other types of savings?<br>RECORD IN FULL | 408 |
| b | And what would you say are the <u>disadvantages</u> of saving with a credit union?<br>RECORD IN FULL | 409 |
| c | Thinking about both the credit union and other types of savings, do you think you now save more or less, altogether, than you would have done if you hadn't joined? | 410 |

Much more    1

A bit more    2

About the same    3

Less    4

## Uses of Credit

SHOW CARD D

17a   Which one of these statements comes closest to how <u>you</u> personally feel about buying things on credit?      411

Never a good thing (you should save up and buy only what you have the cash for)    1

Occasionally necessary (for expensive but essential things you don't have the cash for)    2

A convenient way of buying (you can get things how, and when you want them, instead of having to wait, save or carry losts of cash)    3

A sensible way of buying (it helps you manage your money, improve your living standards or beat inflation)    4

Don't know/none of these    X

SHOW CARD E

18a On this card there is a list of ways of arranging to buy things on credit.
Could you look through the list and tell me:

(i)...which of these types of credit purchase have you (or your husband/wife)
used within the past 12 months, that is, since last ____ (NAME MONTH)? PROBE
Any others? CODE AS MANY AS APPLY

(ii)...which of these types of credit purchase would you prefer to use? PROBE
Any others? CODE AS MANY AS APPLY

(iii)...and which of them would you rather not use if you could avoid it?
PROBE Any others? CODE AS MANY AS APPLY

|  | Used in past year 412 | Prefer to use 413 | Rather not use 414 |
|---|---|---|---|
| Obtaining credit on an Access or Barclay card | 1 | 1 | 1 |
| Hire purchase or credit sale | 2 | 2 | 2 |
| Buying on instalments from a mail order catalogue | 3 | 3 | 3 |
| Having a credit account with a store | 4 | 4 | 4 |
| Buying on instalments from a door to door salesman (or tallyman) | 5 | 5 | 5 |
| Buying on credit from the electricity or gas board | 6 | 6 | 6 |
| None of these | 7 | 7 | 7 |

b) Can you give me the details of your recent purchases?

| CREDIT PURCHASE | 1 | 2 | 3 | 4 |
|---|---|---|---|---|
|  | 415 | 416 | 417 | 418 |
| TYPE OF CREDIT |  |  |  |  |
|  | 419 | 420 | 421 | 422 |
| TYPE OF ITEM PURCHASED |  |  |  |  |
|  | 423,26 | 427,30 | 431,34 | 435,38 |
| PRICE OF ITEMS £ |  |  |  |  |
|  | 439,41 | 442,44 | 445,47 | 448,50 |
| RATE OF REPAYMENT £ |  |  |  |  |
|  | 451 | 452 | 453 | 454 |
| per week | 1 | 1 | 1 | 1 |
| per fortnight | 2 | 2 | 2 | 2 |
| per month | 4 | 4 | 4 | 4 |
| other periods | 8 | 8 | 8 | 8 |

- 14 -

SHOW CARD F

19a On this card there is a list of ways of obtaining a cash loan. Could you look through the list and tell me:

(i)...which of these types of loan have you (or your husband/wife) obtained within the past 12 months, that is, since last _____ (NAME MONTH)? PROBE Any others? CODE AS MANY AS APPLY

(ii)...which of these types of loans would you prefer to use? PROBE Any others? CODE AS MANY AS APPLY

(iii)...and which of them would you rather not use if you could avoid it? PROBE Any others? CODE AS MANY AS APPLY

|  | Used in past year | Prefer to use | Rather not use |
|---|---|---|---|
|  | 455 | 456 | 457 |
| A loan from the credit union | 1 | 1 | 1 |
| A loan or overdraft from a bank | 2 | 2 | 2 |
| A second mortgage from a building society | 3 | 3 | 3 |
| A loan from a finance house or loan company | 4 | 4 | 4 |
| A loan from a moneylender or pawnbroker | 5 | 5 | 5 |
| Check or voucher trading (eg the Provident) | 6 | 6 | 6 |
| None of these | 7 | 7 | 7 |

IF ANY (NON-CREDIT UNION) LOANS IN PAST YEAR
b) Can you give me the details of the loans you have had?

| LOAN | 1 | 2 | 3 | 4 |
|---|---|---|---|---|
|  | 458 | 459 | 460 | 461 |
| SOURCE OF LOAN |  |  |  |  |
|  | 462,65 | 466,69 | 470,73 | 474,77 |
| SIZE OF LOAN £ |  |  |  |  |
|  | 505 | 506 | 507 | 508 |
| PURPOSE |  |  |  |  |
|  | 509,11 | 512,14 | 515,17 | 518,20 |
| RATE OF REPAYMENT £ |  |  |  |  |
|  | 521 | 522 | 523 | 524 |
| per week | 1 | 1 | 1 | 1 |
| per fortnight | 2 | 2 | 2 | 2 |
| per month | 4 | 4 | 4 | 4 |
| other periods | 8 | 8 | 8 | 8 |

(CARD 5)

20a In the past 12 months, have you ever tried to borrow money or buy on credit and been refused?

|  | | 525 |
|---|---|---|
|  | Yes | 1 |
|  | No | 2 | Q21

IF YES
b) Could you tell me about that? RECORD FULL DETAILS

526

- 15 -

## Credit Union Loans

21a  (Can I just check,) have you ever had a loan <u>from the credit union</u>? PROBE How many loans have you had from the credit union since you joined? (And what about your husband/wife?)

| | Resp't 527 | Spouse 528 | |
|---|---|---|---|
| No loans from credit union | 0 | 0 | |
| Has had loan(s) NUMBER | | | c |

IF NO LOANS
b) Is there any particular reason why you have not had a loan from the credit union? RECORD IN FULL, THEN SKIP TO Q24 — 529

IF HAS HAD LOAN(S), IDENTIFY <u>LAST</u> OCCASION (RESPONDENT <u>OR</u> SPOUSE):
c) Could you tell me a bit more about your (last) loan from the credit union?
(i) Did you borrow a fixed amount, or arrange to be allowed to borrow up to a maximum?                                                                                530

|                    |     |
|--------------------|-----|
| Fixed amount       | 1   |
| Up to maximum      | 2   |

531,34

(ii) How much money did you borrow (did you actually draw)?                          £

(iii) Was the money to <u>pay for something you needed</u>, or to <u>pay back money you already owed</u>? PROBE Could you explain what that was?                535

(iv) Are you still repaying the loan, or have you finished paying it off?      536

|                 |   |
|-----------------|---|
| Still paying    | 1 |
| Finished        | 2 |

(v) How much are (were) your repayments on the loan?                         537,39

£

|                 | 540 |
|-----------------|-----|
| per week        | 1   |
| per fortnight   | 2   |
| per month       | 4   |
| other periods   | 8   |

(vi) Do you know what rate of interest they charge(d) on the loan?         541,42

|                          |    |
|--------------------------|----|
| Knows rate of interest % |    |
| Doesn't know             | 99 |

SHOW CARD G
(vii) How do (did) you pay the instalments: do (did) you pay over cash, or is (was) it deducted from pay, or what? PROBE TO CODE                          543

|                                                  |   |
|--------------------------------------------------|---|
| Cash/cheque taken to collection point            | 1 |
| Cash/cheque collected from your home             | 2 |
| Cash/cheque posted to union                      | 3 |
| Standing order from bank/building society        | 4 |
| Deduction from earnings paid direct to union     | 5 |

- 16 -

ALL WITH A CREDIT UNION LOAN

22  a) When you took out a loan from the credit union, how did you go about
    applying for it?
    RECORD IN FULL

544

b) How did they assess your application? Did someone come to see you, or did
you have to talk to a committee, or what?
RECORD IN FULL, AND PROBE How did you feel about that?

545

c) Did you obtain the full amount that you'd applied for, or did they limit
you to less than that?

546

| | |
|---|---|
| Full amount applied for | 1 |
| Limited to less than that | 2 |

d) Did they ask for someone to guarantee the loan for you, in case you didn't
pay?

547

| | |
|---|---|
| Yes, asked for guarantor | 1 |
| No | 2 |

e) On the whole, how happy were you with the way the credit union dealt with
your application for a loan? Were you ... READ OUT

548

| | | |
|---|---|---|
| Very happy | 1 | 8 |
| Fairly happy | 2 | 8 |
| Rather unhappy | 3 | |
| Very unhappy | 4 | |

IF RATHER OR VERY UNHAPPY
f) Why do you say that?
RECORD IN FULL

549

ALL WITH A LOAN; SHOW CARD H
g) If you had not obtained a loan from the credit union, what do you think
you would have done instead? Could you choose an answer from this card?

550

| | | |
|---|---|---|
| ...borrowed the money from somewhere else | 1 | Q23 |
| purchased the items on credit from a shop | 2 | Q23 |
| drawn on your savings with the credit union | 3 | |
| drawn on other savings | 4 | |
| paid cash from weekly or monthly money | 5 | Q23 |
| OR would you not have bought the items you needed? | 6 | Q23 |

IF WOULD HAVE DRAWN CREDIT UNION OR OTHER SAVINGS
h) Why did you decide to take out a loan, rather than use your savings?
RECORD IN FULL

551

ALL WITH A CREDIT UNION LOAN

23  a) Have you ever had any difficulty maintaining the repayments on a loan from
the credit union — either the loan you've just told me about, or any other?
PROBE TO CODE                                                          552

|  |  |  |
|---|---|---|
| No difficulties | 1 | d |
| Difficulties finding money, but no missed payments | 2 | d |
| One or two missed payments | 3 | |
| Several missed payments | 4 | |
| Unable to repay loan | 5 | |

IF ANY MISSED PAYMENTS (CODES 3 - 5)
b) What happened when you missed payments on your loan? What did the credit
union do? RECORD IN FULL                                               553

c) How did you feel about that? RECORD IN FULL                         554

Q24

IF NO MISSED PAYMENTS (CODES 1 - 2 AT a)
d) Do you know what would happen if you missed payments on a loan? What
would the credit union do?
RECORD IN FULL                                                         555

ALL RESPONDENTS

24a  Have you ever asked the credit union for a loan, and been refused? PROBE How
many times has that happened? (PROBE: And what about your husband/wife?)

|  | Resp't | Spouse |  |
|---|---|---|---|
|  | 556 | 557 | |
| No, never been refused | 0 | 0 | Q25 |
| Has been refused NUMBER | | | |

IF HAS EVER BEEN REFUSED
b) Could you tell me about that (on the last occasion)? How much did you ask
to borrow?                                                            558,61

AMOUNT £

c) What did you need the money for: was it to buy something you needed, or to
pay money you already owed?
RECORD IN FULL                                                        562

Q24 CONTINUES ON NEXT PAGE

- 18 -

SHOW CARD I
24   d) Do you know what the reason was, why you could not have that loan. Was it any of the reasons on this card?     563

             ... you had not been saving long enough to qualify     1

          ... you were asking for more than you were allowed to borrow     2

     ... they didn't approve of what you were going to spend the money on     3

      ... you had already borrowed from them as much as they'd allow     4

           ... they weren't sure you'd pay back the money     5

             ... they were short of money to lend out     6

                OR   some other reason     7

                EXPLAIN_____

e) On the whole, how happy were you with the way the credit union dealt with your application for a loan? Were you ... READ OUT     564

                    Very happy     1     8

                   Fairly happy     2     8

               Rather unhappy     3

                 Very unhappy     4

IF RATHER OR VERY UNHAPPY
f) Why do you say that? RECORD IN FULL     565

SHOW CARD J
g) What did you do when you didn't get the loan from the credit union. Could you choose an answer from this card?     566

                ...borrow the money from somewhere else     1

             purchase the items on credit from a shop     2

           draw on your savings with the credit union     3

                   draw on other savings     4

          pay cash from weekly or monthly money     5

         OR did you not buy the items you needed?     6

25a.  What would you say are the <u>advantages</u> for people who borrow from the credit union, compared with other ways of getting credit?
RECORD IN FULL     567

b.  And what would you say are the <u>disadvantages</u> of borrowing from the credit union?
RECORD IN FULL     568

c.  Thinking about both the credit union and other types of credit, do you think you now use more credit or less, altogether, than you would have done if you hadn't joined the union?     569

                    Much more     1

                    A bit more     2

               About the same     3

                      Less     4

## Overview

**26a** Have you ever asked the credit union for financial advice?

|  |  |
|---|---|
|  | 570 |
| Yes | 1 |
| No | 2 |   d

IF YES
**b)** What sort of problem did you need help with?
RECORD IN FULL

571

**c)** Were you pleased with the advice they gave, and the way they offered it?
RECORD IN FULL

572

**d.** Are there any other services which you think the credit union should provide for its members? RECORD IN FULL

573

---

**27a.** Would you say the credit union has made it easier or more difficult for you and your family to manage on the money you get? Or has it made no difference? PROBE TO CODE

574

| | |
|---|---|
| Much easier | 1 |
| a bit easier | 2 |
| made no difference | 3 |
| a bit more difficult | 4 |
| much more difficult | 5 |

**b.** Are you personally interested in the credit union mainly because it can be useful to you; or are you interested mainly in the help it can give to other members?

575

| | |
|---|---|
| Useful to respondent | 1 |
| Help to other members | 2 |

**c.** Some credit union members have told us that they feel put under an obligation to save more than they really want to. Others say thay don't feel under any obligation, either way. How do you feel? PROBE TO CODE BELOW

**d** Some credit union members have told us that they feel put under an obligation to borrow more than they really want to. Others say thay don't feel under any obligation, either way. How do you feel? PROBE TO CODE BELOW

| | Save | Borrow |
|---|---|---|
| | 576 | 577 |
| Feel under strong obligation | 1 | 1 |
| Feel under slight ubligation | 2 | 2 |
| No obligation really | 3 | 3 |
| Definitely no obligation | 4 | 4 |

- 20 -

| | | |
|---|---|---|
| 28a. | Do you intend to remain in the credit union, or are you likely to leave? | 578 |
| | Will definitely stay | 1 |
| | Will probably stay | 2 |
| | Will probably leave | 3 |
| | Will definitely leave | 4 |
| b. | Are there any other improvements that you think could be made to the credit union, that we have not already talked about?<br>RECORD IN FULL | 579 |
| c. | Have you any other comments at all?<br>RECORD IN FULL | 580 |

(CARD 6

## Background Information

| | | |
|---|---|---|
| 29a | Thank you very much for answering my questions. Before I go, I need to ask just a few more details about yourself, so that we can compare whether different types of people have different experiences of credit unions. Can you tell me your age last birthday?<br>RECORD AGE | 605,06 |
| b | CODE MAN OR WOMAN | 607 |
| | Man | 1 |
| | Woman | 2 |

| | | |
|---|---|---|
| 30a. | Can I ask what religion or denomination you belong to? | 608 |
| | Protestant denominations      Church of England | 1 |
| | Methodist | 2 |
| | Presbyterian/Church of Scotland | 3 |
| | Baptist | 4 |
| | Other _____ | 5 |
| | Catholic | 6 |
| | Other religion or denomination _____ | 7 |
| | None | 8 |
| | | 609 |
| b. | CARD K<br>CODE GROUP | ▢ |

- 21 -

| | | |
|---|---|---|
| 31a | Do you have any children living with you? IF YES How old are they? | 610,14 |
| | RECORD NUMBERS OF CHILDREN BY AGE GROUP                     Under 5 | |
| | 6 to 10 | |
| | 11-15 | |
| | 16+ (STILL AT SCHOOL) | |
| | 16+ (LEFT SCHOOL, LIVING HERE) | |
| | IF ANY CHILDREN<br>b) Does your child (do any of your children) belong to the credit union as a junior member? | |
| | RECORD NUMBER OF JUNIOR MEMBERS | 615 |
| | None | 0 |
| c. | Apart from you (and your husband/wife (and children)), do any other adults live here in this household? | 616 |
| | Yes (NUMBER) | |
| | No | 0 |
| | IF OTHER ADULTS<br>d) Who is mainly responsible for the household? PROBE TO IDENTIFY HOH | 617 |
| | Respondent or spouse is HoH | 1 |
| | Other adult is HoH | 2 |
| | e) Does he/she (do they) also belong to the credit union as (a) separate member(s)? | 618 |
| | RECORD NUMBER OF OTHER ADULT MEMBERS | |
| | None | 0 |
| f. | Have there been any important changes in your family in the past year - that is since last _____ MONTH?<br>RECORD CHANGES IN FULL | 619 |

f

| | | | | | |
|---|---|---|---|---|---|
| 32a | Do you own or rent this house/flat? PROBE TO CODE | | | 620 | |
| | Owner-occupied – with mortgage to pay | | | 1 | |
| | – outright | | | 2 | d |
| | Rented – from council | | | 3 | c |
| | – private (unfurnished) | | | 4 | c |
| | – private (furnished) | | | 5 | c |

IF HAS MORTGAGE TO PAY
b) How much do you have to pay for the mortgage (plus insurance on the mortgage)? RECORD IN GRID BELOW, THEN GO TO d)

IF RENTS
c) How much rent do you have to pay. RECORD IN GRID BELOW

ASK ALL
d  Do you have to pay rates (as well as the rent/mortgage you've just mentioned)?

| EXPENSE | Mortgage 621,23 | Rent 624,26 | Rates 627,29 |
|---|---|---|---|
| £ | | | |
| | 630 | 631 | 632 |
| per week | 1 | 1 | 1 |
| per fortnight | 2 | 2 | 2 |
| per month | 4 | 4 | 4 |
| per quarter | 5 | 5 | 5 |
| other periods | 8 | 8 | 8 |
| EXPLAIN _____ | | | |

| | | |
|---|---|---|
| 33 | Finally, we'd like to compare how different people have made use of the credit union. Would you agree to allow the union to let us have details of your account there? This would be in complete confidence, of course? OBTAIN RESPONDENT'S SIGNATURE ON RELEASE FORM IF AGREES, AND CODE RESULT | 633 |
| | Permission given | 1 |
| | Not given | 2 |

| | |
|---|---|
| | 634,36 |
| Time interview completed _____    RECORD MINUTES DURATION | |

- 23 -